THE PRAYERFUL

KISS

A Collection of Prose and Poetry

Francis Etheredge

En Route Books & Media, LLC
St. Louis, MO

⊕*ENROUTE*
Make the time

En Route Books and Media, LLC
5705 Rhodes Avenue
St. Louis, MO 63109

Cover credit: TJ Burdick

Library of Congress Control Number: 2019946039

ISBN-13: 978-1-7325949-4-4
ISBN-10: 1-7325949-4-5

Table of Contents

Preface by Helen Williams i

General Introduction 1

    A Reader-Writer Dialogue 4
    Joseph: Husband of Mary, *Mother of The Son* 5

Zwaddi: Photograph

Part I: Today 7

    The Prayerful Kiss..8
    A Philosophical Psalm 139..............................11
    Christ 14

Part II: Spiralling Upwards?..............................15

The Four Seasons 17
    Autumn Triptych (I) 18
    Timothy Eberly: Photograph

    Winter's Frosty Days (II) 25
    Rodion Kutsaev: Photograph

    Spring-a-Light (III); and 28
    Fotografierende: Photograph

    Summer Clothes Us All (IV) 32
    Gozha Net: Photograph

Firesam: Photograph

Part III: Searching..35

A Trilogy in Search of Self
    Running Speech (I)...............................37
    Particularism (II); and 39
    Water from the Rock (III)....................41
Why Did I Look?..................................43
Dew..45

G. D. Bebeau: Photograph

Part IV: Pain and Joy 49
    Indelible...54
    Suicide 57
    Hidden...60
    The Prayer in our Search for Work 62
    Losing her 64
    Freezing 67
    The Family Tree..................................69

Victoriano Izquierdo: Photograph

Part V: Passing Through 71
    Psalm 151...72
    Loneliness 74
    Mud...76
    The Friend..77
    In the Church Wood.............................78
    Experience..80
A Trilogy of a Kind
    Grape Juice (I)....................................82
    Blossom (II)..84
    The Question (III) 87

Dung Anh: Photograph

Part VI: Writing 90
    My Words Bled...92
    Day-Broken-Bread 93
    Word-Lights 95
    The Gambler..97
    A Bluesy Day...99
    I Wrote...100
    Word-Work 102
    After-words 105
    Without Words...107

Robert J. Soper: Photograph

Part VII: Christ and His Church 110

Exhausting Human Experience Trilogy
    Part I: The Endless Cycle of "Relationships"...........112
    Part II: Psychological, Philosophical and Theological Answers
....115
    Part III: The Answer of God in Action......................118

A Crib Trilogy
    Christmas (I)..120
    A Christmas Present (II)...121
    The Children's Gift (III)..124

Ecumenism (2002) 125
An Angel 127
The Domestic Church...130
Oh Flaming Fire 132
Let us Pray..134
Evangelization...136
About the Author...139

PREFACE

by

Helen Williams

We all have in us a natural desire for everlasting life. We have only to consider our general hope in medical and scientific advances to see a widespread expectation that our lives can be extended. We glimpse the longing to possess life that does not end. However, at a personal level, the desire or longing is clouded, even eclipsed, by pain and suffering so that our journey through life on earth can be a sorry struggle of carrying the baggage we began to accumulate at conception when we inherited our parents' genes.

It took me too many years to realize that we cannot journey alone to maturity. We can be with people all the time but unless we interact with them with all the dignity and depth that human relationships require, then we will not grow into fullness of life. As Francis describes in this work, we can follow many paths, do many potentially useful things and yet not experience fulfilment. We need to discover the right starting point, the heart, the anchor point from which we can risk the search for the answer to two vital questions:

Who am I?

What is the purpose of my life? (What am I to do?)

For me, all my life, Jesus Christ has been the anchor. His Word in Scripture has been a light for me in various dark places because, of course, I have free will. I have not listened very well. There have been unrealistic decisions taken in arrogance or times of rebellion. Through all this, as through Francis' experiences, Jesus has been faithful; his love for me was always there even when I did not realise it; his hand has guided me to listen again and again to his Word of hope and of the promise of eternal life in Him. All this has been in the context of my family life and of the blessings of being part of a Christian Community.

So, I have been called into life to witness to the great love he has for each and every person. This is not a solo mission. I am part of the Church, the family of God, the Body of Christ the Light of the world. Together, and always in precariousness, we reach out to enlighten others.

I hope you will enter into Francis' journey as he writes in poetry and prose. Follow where he leads, and you may find some of your own experiences explained in words that you could not form for yourself. I admire the way he can look at something very ordinary and make of it a new and interesting thought. The gift is akin to that of a great artist of the word as well of pictures, G.K. Chesterton, of whom Ian Ker writes:

Chesterton's philosophy of wonder at and gratitude for existence is well known ... Linked ... is his concept of the role of imagination in enabling us to see the familiar afresh, as it were for the first time. (Ian Ker, G.K. Chesterton, *A Biography*, Preface, OUP, 2011)

GENERAL INTRODUCTION

The suffering that isolates us is an injury to our very being;[1] indeed, it is an indirect way of discovering how profoundly we exist as a being-in-relation[2]: a child; a grandson; a husband; a father; a friend; a workman; and many other aspects of our "whole identity".

As a young man, away at university and unable to accept the study of a psychology that seemed to ignore the very depths of human meaning and existence that had already spoken to me, acknowledging at the same time that it was my fault for not looking into the course more carefully, I was unable to communicate the depth of disappointment and anguish that filled me yet again as yet again there seemed to be no way out of the maze of self-ignorance. The lonely walks on the beach, almost finding in the vast expanse of sky, sea and empty beach a terrible echo of the emptiness within: an emptiness of relationships; indeed, looking back, there is almost nothing as painful as the inability to make friends,

---

[1] My gratitude to Mr. Martin Higgins, MA, for his unfailing help throughout the years and for proof-reading yet another work.

[2] Cf. *The Human Person: A Bioethical Word*, published at: http://enroutebooksandmedia.com/bioethicalword/.

1

socialize, discover that "connectedness" that brings an unfolding of being that we cannot do without.

The whole me, then, is not an abstract entity made up of parts, whether it be "body and soul", "biological, psychological and social characteristics" or "male, person and human"; rather, the whole me is both elusive and like an apple: the bruise impacts the whole fruit and, while it can be cut away, the cutting away is an irreversible change in the reality of the whole apple. In other words, even in the small events of life, I am wholly involved. Indeed, even when I go out into the front garden to see the children off to school, it is impossible not to feel the fear that seeing them off on their bikes brings with it - the fear and the prayer for their safety. At the same time there is always a change to notice among the plants. One plant is wrapping a "wavy" strand of stem around another plant, like the curling of a glass rod as it receives the heat, so one plant has "touched" and wrapped itself around another as it grows, showing its sensitivity to the presence of another. The children and I notice this and other aspects of the garden in the few moments before they are gone.

We underestimate ourselves completely if we just think in terms of the individualistic presence of each of us in the universe. Rather, we are like these plants, linking with one another, discovering that the presence of the other is as necessary as the very fact of our own existence. What we experience, then, is the mystery of not so much being a fruit, open to bruising, as that our "connectedness" both brings us into the innumerable events and interests of the day while bringing with it a kind of vulnerability. The suffering of being alone is a kind of spiralling down into a shrivelling isolation; but, conversely, there is a suffering which accompanies us in being with others, making us both grateful and prayerful.

Marriage and family life, as simple as they are, multiply the mystery of being me in ways that makes one realize that relationships open us up to a whole world of interactions which reverberate, almost like a sound in circulation, between enjoying what others bring and sharing, or seeking, or praying that what impacts on them, that impacts on me, will be helpfully lived between us.

The landscape, then, populated by so many people, is a place of encountering others. Walking on an empty beach is not so much about an agonizing loneliness as the heart of man discovering, deeper than we realize, that our planet is a place of meeting; and, in His own way, our Saviour walks among us to rebuild the brokenness that breaks the heart, not just the isolated heart, but the heart that exists between us and suffers in the isolation of its members.

In summary, praying through difficulties showed in the times of unemployment becoming opportunities for research and writing as a part of further study, resigning from a position which shrank to an unrecognizable redefinition of what it was has now given writing the opening it needed. Unprofitability has encouraged me to work more collaboratively and to embrace the challenge of almost aphoristic summaries of experience or short, possibly translucent, "reality bites".

This book "takes in" many different experiences and, I hope, takes us through the possibility that pain and darkness are the "last word". Even if, going through "dead ends" is excruciatingly slow and impossible, fully, to describe, I nevertheless hope that it is possible to find that thread of life which, slight as it is, is stronger than the gravitational crush of black holes: the prayer beads that lead, like lights in a dangerously thick fog which hides the precipitous edges and pits into which we plunge.

While prayer, then, is not the preoccupation of this book; it is prayer that makes it possible: that makes possible the daily life that unfolds "life to the full" (cf. Jn: 10: 10); and, just as in the life of Joseph, the events of life bring a good not of our making, that transcends our own plans, bursting beyond us a word for others.

A Reader-Writer Dialogue

In view, however, of the final structure of this book, it maybe that this can be a help to reading it through your own life; and, therefore, it was written in three ways. The first drafting was at different times and in different ways and, at the same time, the bits and pieces of this collection were amassed, eventually, into a ring-binder. Secondly there was a first attempt at a collection of poems which never saw publication but did include pieces which had been published. Then there was the possibility of bringing the collection together, again, and adding prose passages; the whole idea of which came from reading a few pieces publicly and noting that there was often a brief introduction of each piece – a method I copied.

Finally: there was adding pictures to relieve the text-only content of the book. It was while resolving the formatting problems of doing this that I began to think that maybe the "spaces" in the book could be for the reader's own response, odd poetry, collected pictures; and, therefore, there arose the possibility of a reader-writer dialogue ... .

JOSEPH: HUSBAND OF MARY, MOTHER OF THE SON

An angel made known to me
your child is
The Son of God made man
in you
and given to us.

With God in you beginning
Who now through you is coming:

He gave to me my manhood
to give to you a husband
and a father to your child.

I suffered who it was you were
until He gave me to know
that your motherhood
was a mystery clothed at His birth:
You are the Mother of our God.

How can I say what grew in me
as I saw Him stretch your tent?
Can a mystery sown in you
spring faith in me?

Is this the meaning of our marriage:
to be one openness to Life?

Oh what silence broke
when His breath
sang out that night!
He came from the root of our people,
an infant king of His kingdom,
and we wrapped Him in praise
of His family of man.

THE DAWNING TODAY[3]

We live in the present – even if the past seems to be too present or the future diminishes our time to pause because of the pressing deadlines, schedules and bills and all the other myriad impacts on "today". Today is still that moment we are given and, as it is always with us, it is a taste of eternity; however, it is also where we are with all that life entails: what we have experienced, thought, tried and failed, tried again and persevered with. More importantly, perhaps, today is where the love of God has brought us along with the community of people He has carried on the same time-tide as we are on. But I know from experience that if there is no prayer there is no dawning of the day – only the dread of what is to come and the difficulties ahead. Make prayer the breakfast of the day.

---

3 Zwaddi: Free use of photographs from the following website: https://unsplash.com/photos/YvYBOSiBJE8. I have generally written my own titles to the pictures. I would, however, like to record my gratitude to those who made their work available for free, either on a website for this purpose or who have given written consent to use their work. Thank you.

PART I

TODAY

These poems, beginning with "A Prayerful Kiss", are about that pilgrimage from loneliness to connectedness. Indeed, the first poem is about that law of attraction that runs throughout the universe becoming personalized in men and women. How can a kiss not be a prayerful activity if it is indeed the giving of love: a gentle giving that does not steal what is not being given? Did the Creator of the whole universe write the kiss upon the lips of lovers to show and to shower the world in "moments" bursting into flower – telling transparently that the existence of the kiss is a "sign" that we are "beings-for-love"?! Can a mechanistic, functional account of the kiss tell us about the root involvement of our whole being in the "momentary" passing of touches too touching to stay still; and, like the passing of a current with that dynamic that belongs to love, leading us more deeply into an openly generous embrace?

So what can claim to be a science that does not do justice to the reality of physicality, physiology, psychology, philosophy and theology in a wholesome account of the mysterious existence of the almost scriptural concreteness of the person-expressing-body-language-of-lips?

THE PRAYERFUL KISS

How many particles wizz without a sound, whirl effortlessly,
bind and build structures impossible to describe, hidden,
multiplying a multiplicity of shapes and sizes,
attracting and repelling, stable and changing,
emerging, in time, visibly magnificent?

Particles, partnered in tension, like static,
building in the atmosphere,
striking in a lightening, leaping between earth's arising,
wavering tendrils,
and the massing in the air, tingeing mauve, almost smouldering
colours but too pale, electric, arcing between poles, closing the
circuit and running so swiftly fast

to translate into

power, movement, energy, heat, light and a billion trillion
artistic touches
in a brilliantly dancing display of coloured shapes and shaping
colours.

Deep within the depths of all our wondering, arising between
plants and animals,
between insects and flowers, species of all kinds,

like from like, linked through

a common bonding, sparkling with light,
like sparklers in the night,
passing likeness through difference,
like match and tinder:

young springing from old

– new passing through generations leaving their trace and
trailing away, almost ebbing away,
quietly, noiselessly, fading away, then still,
slipping, imperceptibly, into the ground.

What in us comes together if not a universal attraction,
transformed and personalised: speaking; fruitfully suffering;
and enduringly changing through a *Word* rebounding in us from
the beginning and begging us to believe in being poured out in a
poverty that hopes against hope for help.

Wholly unlikely, I know, to believe in the prayerful kiss –
as if the Creator could have created the splendour of the
sky's dawning,
myriad awakenings, and the sweet, barely on the air scents of
flowers,

without disclosing in a million traces, the free gift of an
abundant giving,

a beautiful singing,
of Love being the beginning.

If we gather up many of the points that have been made in
a particular subject and, like a pointillist composition, the art
of painting as if showing the grain of a photograph, maybe the
definition that arises out of this process lies in the
"impression" of the whole rather than in concentrating on one
particular part. Alternatively, maybe there are fewer words
which work, whether slipping in unobtrusively or rising up,
arresting our reading, to open a culture, a time and a place and
allow us to pass "amidst" the fruit of enriching lives, garnering
a more precise definition of our subject. Or perhaps our
research is like concentric circles which, like the rings of a
tree, encompass a whole; however, it not only take time to root
the growth but to amass, too, that wealth of experience which

makes it possible to go right from the peripheries of life to the centre.

The following piece, drawing on "impressionistic", more precise types of definition and a variety of accounts, is called "A Philosophical Psalm" and is one of the most difficult prose-poems in this whole collection. Indeed, it may be possible to wonder that it is even included in this book. However, the challenge of expressing a summary account of the human being means that, whatever its difficulties, it brings together a life-time's work in seeking to understand and to express the mystery of human personhood. The reference in the title to Psalm 139 acknowledges a debt to the marvellous work and nature of Scripture; and, in particular, to the biblical "imagination" striving to communicate one of the clearest answers to one of the most challenging questions: When does each one of us begin?

A PHILOSOPHICAL PSALM 139

Conception
Begins a biologically inscribed psychological development
that unfolds socially.

How else do we describe the indivisibly
Existing being-in-relation,
Begotten through togetherness
Being given existence
in the *Covenant of the flesh*?

Rooted in the Un-Originate God:
Adam from the ground and Eve from his side,
both communicating the dynamic difference of the
Mystery of the Person.

Conceived in Christ from conception,
saved in the reciprocal self-giving of Christ and His Church,
Through the Cross of Love's own choosing –
Called from Love to love.

And

Where the body lives, there is the soul,
and where both are is the person.

What is inward informs what is outward!
What is outward points inward!
What is invisible is made visible!

And

Where the body lives, there is the soul,
and where both are is the person.

Meaning, arising from the beginning,

Breathed again in each of us,
Takes up what is "within" and "without",
Mingling myriad impressions and possibilities,
New and old, insights ancient and modern,
Spoken, written, sung, painted, sculpted and designed,
Dialoguing from beginning to end,
In the depth and breadth
Of time and eternity.

The complete individual
is inseparably cultural!

And

Where the body lives, there is the soul,
and where both are is the person.

In the very being of the human person
is the expression of a word:

person "from" Person;
life "from" Love;
"from" Communion to Communion.

Love Unbegotten begetting
a beginning of each of us:
We are an Icon
of the Beginning.

I married in 1996 and, in one sense, wonder how it was that I did not write about marrying, especially in view of over twenty years of searching about what to do with my life; and, as I have said elsewhere, discovering that I could no more marry than put my head in a bear-trap. What, then, is the relevance of this poem about Christ? Christ came to the wedding feast at Cana not, it seems, as an afterthought about

12

marriage but in view of the very reality of marriage entailing His presence. In other words, the very mystery of marriage makes present the turning water into wine: our sufferings into joys. Christ comes, in other words, into the very reality of relationships which are always in need of renewal.

Even if "Who" Christ is remains, in a way, inexpressibly difficult, echoed faintly in the limitations of an account of ourselves, it is nevertheless a part of the writer's pilgrimage to write, every now and then, about the Shepherd who sought him out across the lost years of wandering hither and thither, whether in mountainous places or in "moments" of temptation which turned into years of crushing consequences.

CHRIST[4]

A dropping flame
is sown in the
earth of Mary the sign of man.

The Incarnation builds
a Church out of family life.

Christ,
immersed in the family of man,
is the lamb offering aflame
in the crucifixion.

His blood runs down like boiling gold
and splits the night-cold ground.

His body, baked in affliction,
is scattered like ash in the broken clay:
sown as food in the giving.
His Spirit falls like fire
on dried out hearts
when Pentecost breaks
a mountain into rain.

Beg God our awakening lives
are arms outstretched like Him
in the work of raising a dance to
His blazing return.

---

[4] First published in *The Sower*, January 1996; but slightly changed
in this collection.

PART II

SPIRALLING UPWARDS?

The theme of human identity is explored in terms of the more ordinary language of life and relationships; indeed, the four seasons that characterize our planet are a vehicle for the changes that often appear in our relationships. However, just as the seasons are more pronounced in one country or another, perhaps there are times when our relationships are going through a particular type of change; and, indeed, the point is that a relationship can undergo a variety of seasons and that this is a part of its reality: a natural part of the changes that are an indispensable expression of growth.

Autumn, then, begins the cycle; it was the season of the present in which it was written. Nevertheless, it does not follow that the quartet had to begin with it; indeed, it was the third of "the Seasons" to be written. Autumn, however, offered that sense of enriched aging, of companionship, of the beauty of company and conversation; and, at the same time, it is a season leading to Winter: to the "sleep" before springing into eternal life. Perhaps, too, Autumn is the season in which it is no longer necessary to strive so hard to be what it is impossible to be, successful according to our own criteria, as the beauty of the tree that changes colour is precisely a part of the process of its dying back and slipping into a silhouetted simplicity.

What follows, then, began as a single piece; however, in time, the thread of thoughts almost "insisted" on a three-piece work. The second and third parts took up the theme of imagination, both surreally in the sense of describing imaginative reactions to "moments" and "scenes" but also because of the very suitability, or so it seemed at the time, of a kind of ethereal fieriness that fitted the depiction of death and its transitions: hell; purgatory; and heaven.

THE FOUR SEASONS

5

Pictures, especially "found" pictures, are chosen because of some connection with the prose-poem; however, each picture is its own perception which, in a way, expresses the photographer's relationship to what was seen. Nevertheless, just as words begin with the writer or, better, continue with the writer writing them, so pictures come into a new context and prompt, in their own way, a slightly different point of departure. I can remember, long before writing was probably even considered to be a possibility, heaping up the leaves on the grass and kicking through them until, finally, we had finished burying ourselves in them and playing and dad told us to put them around the roses for compost. We pass on our memories, hopefully, to help others grow.

---

5 Timothy Eberly: https://unsplash.com/photos/HUiNRjXr-bQ.

AUTUMN TRIPTYCH:
AUTUMN IS THE FIERY SEASON (I)

Part I: "Being with Child"

Trees-a-bright with coloured notes: greens amidst yellows, browns
and reds; what poor words for so many flecks of living lights,
ablaze in the dying of the leaves:

what falls of leafy shapes lie scattered, scattering on the breeze,
almost washed up on the side, like cornflakes along the path.

Pavements edged with goblin waste, as if splashing gobs gobbling
stolen soggy cereals,
were washed aside as they rushed through the night-time robbing
of cupboards, shops and tables ready for the morning.

Walking is a way of "being with children", an unfolding of "being
with child" in a wonder-world of imaged impressions, arising
surprising shapes and their suggestions:

almost horses edged in luminous fringes, fuzzy arrow feathered
angels and darkening mood drains and all kinds of "in-betweens".
What of clouds and storms and sudden, overwhelming changes,
looming in the glowering sky,
lowering the sky line and dropping upon us?
Will flood and wind take what is within as well as what is
without?
What remains when what is gone threatens an abandoning of
what is left?
Fruits end as green tomatoes redden on the window ledge,
too late to change on the plant, apples fall and rot the more
terribly the more is wasted, sunflowers lean, head-heavy,
sowing seeds in their splendidly shaped outlandishly
eye-browed eyes,

18

Withering flowers, albeit a few remain, eaten leaves, scarcely green, more
like lime yellow, yet these old plants bear cup upon cup of seeds to fall,
as if a parable of old age in which the failing health of recent years
is a witness to the "worth" of weakness: a prayer full of promises of future ripenings.

Contrast the colourless backs of "phone-heads", turned ever away elsewhere,
towards what "other" sights and sounds than those around,
following whatever fashions billboards, generating conformity:
let us be the distinguished guest of full humanity – a person
brimming with communications "old" and "new".

The older needing interrupted routines and contradicted
un-thought through ways
and the younger needing
what endures and even benefits from engaging with constant
change or is it the other way round?

Like an old married couple, still burning bright,
flaming trees, feathered in their finest plumage, blooming in the sun, shrouded in mist,
dripping in the rain, festive even in the wet,
holding forth a commentary on the slowly silent changes in a life
still sparking togetherness amidst the noise and race of traffic –
still showing forth the treasure of time wasted together:
glimpsing now in eternity.

Part II: Breakfast and other Imaginations

A writing break is a time to sit and go, to read, to see to the
mending of the car, to visit places and to walk and pray.

But, to return to writing, it is a bit like rubbing dirt off a stone,
knocking soil off a root or scrabbling around in the mud and

looking for the trickle of thought amidst the memories
of moaning and groaning and getting out and about:

the moments of light-bright glad we bothered to brave the
resistance to going out.

Does it really belong to autumn words to think of meals on walks?

The crunchy crispy leaves; the dusty dregs of cornflake dust
amidst the flurrying flakes off trees; and the starry starry stark leaf
could be cereal or chocolate shapes, silhouetted against the sky,
while the great green and yellow curtains come down to the very
edges of the water, luminously delightful.

One minute we are together and then a partial silence
as two have become distracted and, as I call,
I hear talking in the trees and imagine the great evergreen taking
its already fallen shape further,
uprooting the barely hidden roots and dropping them into the
water.

How many anxious minutes abound around the climbers, hoping
they enjoy the view but wishing, wishing them down and glad
when feet run down the trunk?

Walking where the trunks of trees rise up like an up-ended
octopus or the fallen, washed and bare remains of a fir looks as if
ready to run, insect like, taking gigantic steps at a time or the
creepy crawly plants that seem, as if mentally, to invade our space
and wave their tendrils while walking towards us –

And the small eared or horned black shape waiting,
up in the woods, as darkening strengthens the contrast of shapes
and, equally, signals the time to go and eat, taking our leave of the
undulating roots that almost move.

We talk of "The wood of transformations" and resist the
creeping sense of dusk coming closer to take our imaginations
a step nearer to being frightening, the writers among us
wondering at the claims becoming too vivid as we almost hurry,

avoiding the slippery slimy soggy muddy boggy messes,
going with granny
along a less slippery path back to the car and home to dinner.

Part III: Final Fires

Winter is coming in with the cold, visible in the chilly light of
day, in the sky filling the growing, gaping gaps left by failing,
falling leaves, staying with the freezing drops on the windscreen.

Three fires spring up in autumn.

There is a cold brightness: a place almost warm but dull – as if
the very warmth had left the light that filled the leaves,
"abstracted" from the love that makes for life.

There is yellow on the rose, not the yellow of vibrant living but
the yellowing from the black dot of death; and, in time, the rose-
spindly goes and the stems die, browning and dropping off.

There is a deadness that does not go before life and the
resurrection; but, in the dying, dies without returning: leafless
stems, thin and brown, supporting disease.

A second fire leads to a third but is for a time its own purely
brightening blaze.
Like the heat that burns off the rot and strips to the bare grain
the original wood even if still slightly
changed by the wear and care of many years. Or the heat that
"fixes" a change but, in the course of it, changes what is to be fixed,
like a glaze that is a kind of glory on the pottery,
sealing it for the gift it carries.

Or the burning that fills the iron but not to melting and radiates from within – remaining "porous" to the pouring heat which spreads outward.

The third fire is a place of gathering, as with the evening brazier in which burns the wood we gathered, the burning brings a meal and changes, irreversibly, the ingredients into a meaning amidst the company of others: a meaning of "being with" that multiplies outwards, like the ringing ripples of a sound, extending an invitation to gather, as around a multitude of hearts, the love that builds, sweeps and swirls like a warm tide or, better, a warmth in the breeze, touching everyone – inexhaustibly embracing.

WINTER[6]

If you look at the frost very closely you will see that each particle of ice, as it were, is built on the one below and that together they make a kind of totem pole facing in different directions, building up into a tower; and, where the frost rises from the exposed rings of a tree, you will see that there are rows of little towers of ice arranged along the curved rings which have arisen from each year's growth.

It takes time, however, to notice what is happening around us. Indeed, that time can come from waiting for another person and, instead of being filled with impatience, moaning and complaining about his or her time keeping, there is an opportunity to observe what exists.

Frost is an image-word-message: a brick with which to build.

"Winter" was in fact the first of what has become the four seasons to be written, followed by "Spring"; but, in the new

---

6 Rodion Kutsaev: https://unsplash.com/photos/QN2BhLmoUJo.

sequence, it comes after "Autumn". It was while thinking of the cold that I remember, distinctly, the painful chill on coming back to a bed-sit from a study-weekend away, surrounded by people, cooked meals, lectures and the comforts of an old religious building with a chapel.

There is no doubt that relationships can draw on the whole range of comparisons with weather, temperature, change, texture and natural forms; and, indeed, like any sequence of changes, there is still the constant theme of what is undergoing the changes: the general nature of estrangement's conversion to intimacy and the particular characteristics that arise and develop within the mystery of marrying and marriage and family life.

The following poem has three movements, as it were, from the familiar to the remembered, from the weather to the withering past experiences and from the evocation of marriage to the barely expressed presence of children.

WINTER'S FROSTY DAYS (II)

Earth like bright cauliflowers in the shade,
Dotted bubbled, studded paths,
White patches on black and grainy roads;

Lopsided ice-stalks, balanced, stand in growing circles,
Spider webs picked out in sparkling chains,
Hard, almost invisible places, stealing steadiness:
The past suddenly present.

Cold, a sudden chilling, like the cold of parting in the sea,
A different kind of freezing to that of pipes,
When lovers part, never having been wholly together,
unable to pass through the barbed gate: the barred gate: marriage.

A loose mist losing difficulties in wet and wishing days:
Easy slipping into vanished moments –
almost spiking hardened veined moments.

In the impenetrable "place" of the heart's abandonment of
hope, God spoke and hope in His Help existed.
Thus was born the marriage miracle of hoping when hope was
hopeless.

A ringed couple, arm in arm, with or without their children;
Walking out of the shadowy cold,
Keeping in the light-side of the street.
Slipping, sometimes, falling together or apart,
Never completely broken, skating a bit, chilled,
Still breathing, two lives living breath by breath;
Prayerfully scraping off creepy crawly insults:
Un-speaking; un-silent speech; un-dead hurts;
Persisting in the warmth of turning back,
Turning past pains, towards a present new,
Hoping, as always, in the coming, coming spring.

SPRING[7]

This year spring did not bring the tulips to life beyond a few leaves and then, accidentally, they were trodden on as a child lost his balance while getting ready to set off on his bike. But, like lap-tops that fall off laps, crockery that breaks, bicycle gears that get twisted into spokes, there are many ways which we can lose the perception of what is beautiful – but turn and look again!

In this third Season of Life, there is a definite focus on what the word almost bursts to say in the very reality of the season itself: "Spring". Then there is the exploration of that which has

---

7 Fotografierende: https://unsplash.com/photos/sxuqoDJf4-s.

"sprung" and entails the very fact of the universe itself, the changes it undergoes and the place it is for changes that beautify us. At the same time, all time seems to be involved in this "beginning and ending" season, suggesting a start but also the reality of passing through beauty to the originally beautiful "place". There is the sense of what was painful being changed, like conversion takes a sword and makes a 'plowshare' (Is 2: 4) or dung, in being compost, is exactly the bed of brilliant changes. In other words, those experiences that bring blushes of humiliation are like pulses of growth in the hands of God, showing the power of the Almighty to lighten our burdens and illuminate our lives with love.

Spring is almost that "paradigmatic" season in which life is lived to the full (cf. Jn 10: 10) betokening that "beatific" transfiguration of the whole of life in a splintering splendour of fragments of light that yet make the presence of a whole and suggest, in a moment, the wonder of a life transformed from within and ablaze without: an impossible hope of the hope that arises out of the hopeless times begetting hope.

We live as if immersed in the day; but, in a moment, we will be flung into eternal flight. Are we flightless beings or are we ready to fly? Will we take flight as if being ready for the unexpected or will we falter in the suddenness of departure? Will our leaving be like a going on what has been given to us or will we be wrenched from what we think is in our hands?

SPRING-A-LIGHT (III)

Almost too lightly,
slightly pulsing waves awash throughout interstellar spaces,
travelling rhythms unimaginable,
light as bright as star-light in the dawning morning,
arriving early, colouring earth's halo,

freshly blushing flowers brightening,
dew dropped, sparkling, warming water,
planting a pulse of growth in a plant,
or clothing, in a moment, a chilly breeze.

Like laden bridesmaids, burgeoning blossoms,
spring before the leaves,
floating from the trees,
swirling in the breeze,
confirm the 'marriage of the Lamb' (Rev 19: 7).

Guest tulips, like cupped light, goblets of blood orange, streaked
with yellow, a standing adoration,
with many other splashing greened plants,
wild and tame,
where no weed is a weed only freshly green,
sprouting a bursting of limp wings,
flocking on branches,
festively gesticulating in every direction.

Out of what furious furnace splashed the impulse of the morning
until, in time, brightness brims o'er the day?

White light splitting through edges,
lifts the hardened wintry weathering off the ground;
and, touching the wounds of frosted, brittle stones,
breaks a hillside into humbler rubble,
rubbishing dizzy heights and levelling hills.

"Oh Mary Magdalen, lest I fall away, let me like you fall to the feet
of the Lord!" (cf. Mt 28: 9)
Spring light sprung alight illuminates the dead dust
and dying corners,
sinking into the squalor a shrivelling intensity as the beams
irradiate the place to rehabilitate in time for Easter's rising:
Love's blazing gaze,
smelting impurity strips hearts
into wholly whole singing lovers.

Arising in song, flowing to the future, a people rises, rising upon a
thermal to the starry entrance hence.

But progress is both seasonal and like the sea:
first the tide takes us and then we slip back;
but then, again, time's-tide takes us in and we go forward.

The dying sky draws us, draining us onward
and into the delving deep through the dwindling light,
drawing us on to untold orchestral sounds and artistic delights
amid the wealth of peoples' playing.

Whence came this light?
Light out of what light sprung the image of itself in sights
and sounding sculptures?
Out of what impenetrably white lightness suddenly spoke
Existence?

Standing visibly forth, creation hints of the staggeringly beautiful,
almost indescribably musical, word untellable,
shape unknowable,
crying out from the hidden depths of light's bursting brilliance –

blasting banality, routine, boredom –
in the breathtaking glimpse of the impossible actuality of God
dressing the wounds which wing us upward,
taking us back to the clouds' bright opening,

intuiting the passage to eternal day.

SUMMER[8]

I particularly remember the long summer holidays stretching away like a long, tiring day. There was the standing around on the cricket field wondering how it was possible that people invented this game of standing under the sun and waiting, endlessly, for something to happen. Or the summer work on a farm, frequently forgetting my lunch and hoping that the farmer would notice and bring me a sandwich; but then, when we were on a field, fetching in the straw particularly, how dry and hot and dusty it was and how my almost only thought was when would we finish.

There were many other experiences but it is striking how those that involved the interminability of time standing seemingly still, still stand out down the many years that have followed; but now, instead of that desert like slowness, there

---

[8] Gozha Net: https://unsplash.com/photos/xDrxJCdedcI.

is the full flood of days of living in a growing family and experiencing time anew – as full and fuller still.

"Summer", in a way, is what I would have expected to be the brightest of the four seasons; but when it came to it there seemed to be very different kinds of experience summed up in the summer months. Each season has its bright and painful times. Perhaps, in a way, the summer is a symbol of those hot and hard working days when, as a boy, I would cycle to work on a farm, dream of love, earn a little money, play tennis and cycle home, often very tired and very often without a regular lunch as thinking ahead seemed a step too far into the future.

Summer, then, is a kind of fullness of life and work but, in being so, a time of exertion, of being stretched across the demands of work and study, evangelization and family life and failing, in all three, to be anything other than the "day-to-day dad", barely managing to make it to work and clinging to prayer like to a raft upon rapids and hoping against hope to hit calmer waters and stress-freer stretches in which to glide and catch a glimpse of growing, talking children and times to read, rest and remember what it is to enjoy "being" and "noticing" the growth of plants and other "every day wonders" which pass, almost too easily, as too ordinarily extraordinary touches of intelligence beyond telling.

SUMMER CLOTHES US ALL (IV)

in the free finery of days tumbling together
or is this a fiction, fixing itself like makeup over boring,
stressful years, seasoned with disappointments?

Pausing, slicing the times apart:
there were months of plain playing,
more colourless than gravestones,
which drained away the time to read and write;
and yet these days were humbly good:
drawing on ordinary games and activities
before reading and writing were unearthed or discovered.

Or what about the dream-loves that dissolved, poignantly, bitterly,
only to stay too long in the longing for them to last until, like glass
bubbles,
their shattering superficiality spearheaded questions about what
attracts beyond the face of flesh?

Or what about the "long-heat" of difficulties,
evaporating easy answers and makeshift solutions,
the persistence of problems that take the temper out of metal,
blunting the hope of resolving anything?

Turning, the divine Shaper who, unexpectedly,
turned to me and gave, freely,
the hope of His creating help.

Then there was the miracle of being married now and struggling in
the heat with the settling of children,
adapting to the changes children bring,
changing with the changes
children's challenges bring,
worrying over everything.

Decades on, scarcely conscious, sitting,
slumped in a sea-side chair,

exhausted from the machinations of work manipulations,
struggling to watch the children running to and fro,
afraid to admit an almost total uselessness as age and weariness
lag behind their dashing through the waves.

Summer is a service:
writing less to be present more;
letting words work between us, core to core,
drawing observations, encouraging imaginations,
mending the hurt of busier times and impossibly
irritated nerve endings;

taking time to walk and talk and stop,
like breathing open thoughts too hidden to be found easily
and too slow for the busy, hurried,
rushed moments of "fitting in" what,
after all, is first of all – the face to face times;
flowers abound but more lovely are the plans
of wife and children,
shrivelling out the temptation to work with innumerable helpings
to do the doing of growing years and improvised happenings,
nullifying the numbing of not doing "my own thingamies".

A season of openness that shows forth
who has been thinking what,
no longer disguised by a few words, silence, or avoiding our
common life;

and then there is gathering: the gifts of turned over thoughts that,
like new shoots, are bright aspects of familiar family life
discovered afresh in unexpected places.
Summer-time has a kind of fulsome beauty,
rewarding winter's work and completing spring's beginnings,
staying the course of the seasons, their setbacks and openings,
unfolding scents and colours, fruits wild and grown,
contemplating Christ and His Church as the image and likeness of
the full-grown man and woman.

AN IMAGE HAS ITS OWN STORY[9]

This picture has the advantage of hiding the person's face; and, in times of pain and difficulty, it is almost possible to say that our face is hidden: the very suffering we experience disguises our full reality. There are times, then, when our lives, like our faces, are more hidden than we realize; and, therefore, the discoveries we make do not necessarily make us happy – but they are necessary if we are to be happy. Happiness, ultimately, is about being loved and being loved is about being loved for the whole person we are. There is only, to my knowledge, one who loves us like this: 'God shows his love for us in that while we were still sinners Christ died for us' (Rom. 5: 8).

---

9 This image is credited to: 'Firesam!' on flickr; no changes made: https://www.flickr.com/photos/firesam/5242760927.

PART III

SEARCHING

How many places, how many conversations, how many beginnings are there to the question of what life is about? But, at the same time, there almost seems to be an accumulation of disappointment as one path leads to yet another junction and other paths and no path seems to lead anywhere longer than going on to another place; however, even in the course of this process there were significant moments which, like some kind of "island" of insight, seemed significant at the time and even enduringly so, but which subsided and left one wondering, almost: So what and what next?

"Running Speech" remembers, as it were, an awakening in the process of leaving childhood and coming into adulthood; and, in so doing, beginning to "inherit" more fully the psychological experience that was actually mine. As, you will see, there was a definite "obstacle" in the flow of the past through the present. I began to realise that I did not know what to do with my life, whereas others seemed to be preparing for university and for work. I started a process of questioning that was like looking for the tracks that would lead me back to a beginning that would help me to go forward; but, in actual fact, it was like there were no footprints in the mud behind me and therefore I had to go looking for the past that did not seem to be present.

I remember, vividly, a cumulating angst; indeed, it was like a kind of "meaning" claustrophobia: as if the very sense of life had slipped and there was an impossibly incommunicable unhappiness. Unhappiness is almost like an injury which, untreated, becomes life-threateningly burdensome; indeed, the very settling of unhappiness is already indicative of an injury that, being internal, is like a slow growing suffocation. Our hearts need to breathe their emotions and reactions and, in the process, the meaning needs to surface like coming up for air and gasping for breath again. But tragically contradictory is the need to speak and the inability to say what needs to be spoken; and, therefore, the cycle of life-as-communication as well as the "reception-of-experience" is broken. There is a hiddenness, then, like a meaning-vacuum, that collapses the walls through which our lives pass; unless, in an uncertain but searching way, we stumble on the dam and start undoing the doing that is done.

A TRILOGY IN SEARCH OF SELF (I)
RUNNING SPEECH

As
a child
I swore myself to silence:
it rose over reason and dried in my throat.

Humiliation, like a wedge driven down, brought division.

Did you ever build a dam:
pile it high and make it deep,
build it up and break it down,
lose the hours and even sleep?

But play can beget
the dream of older years
and grow in us the secret which,
when ripe, opens out at night
the reason for my living sleep;

and like a breaking down,
my life, built up behind the dam,
pours through the sand
a route of running speech
which, once found,
discovers in its bed the
I of me.

In the second part of this trilogy there is a transition between a more psychological account of experience and the tendency to think, philosophically, that life has a kind of "natural path", almost like the path of a particle down the "electro-magnetic veins" of the universe. In a certain sense, there does seem to be some merit to these thoughts of a "natural path"; indeed, the following piece has drawn upon a

Zen Buddhist story which exhorts us to be patient in the search for self: a kind of active waiting as we watch for the swirling water to still. The problem I experienced was that due to the impulse to travel, to go somewhere else and to do something different, there did not seem "to be time" to be still; and, in general, while my first attempt to live in one place for five years, failed at three, there was a second period which went on to the full five years which followed it. It was during that five-year period that I worked through various courses on teaching design, playing various instruments, mathematics, philosophy, psychology, law, fine art and, finally, the beginnings of theology. It was during this time that the memory of once enjoying a discussion in school on the subject of baptism, indeed "Who can baptize?", indicated an interest I had not noticed or had neglected to pursue.

The course, a kind of supplementary introduction to the teachings of the *Catholic Church* for those in teaching or training to teach, turned into the beginnings of a life-long search of the mysteries of the Catholic Faith. In a certain sense, then, having "exhausted" various kinds of enquiry about my health, the possibility of teaching, there emerged demanding questions about truth, which led on from a kind of philosophical to a theological pursuit of truth. Thus, having discovered a path of interest it did seem to progress, albeit very fitfully, on an exploration of what, up to that point, I had not intended to pursue.

A TRILOGY IN SEARCH OF SELF (II)
"PARTICULARISM"

If the bank is broken –
how will the river live?

Living like flooding water
is like running out-of-one-route
into nowhere.

Who can drain the land
and restore the river's course?

A monk advised me to travel –
until travelling taught me to stand still.

Now I have stopped travelling,
the water in the bowl can stop swirling
-but it does not and bubbles burst the first stillness –
and seeing their reflections
obscures the reflection I have striven almost all
my running years to find.

The self is simple – but seeing our self is not.

But if the bowl springs an overflowing,
like a singing in the hillside,
then a new course of action
can an old path uncover.

And while a stream is not a river
-hope is in the trickling word –
because the root it will travel
is like the acorn to the tree,
the smoke of several field fires that funnel in the sky,
or the flight of the light-wave-particle

in the grain of every space

and we will be led, where lost we did not go,
if we will be led, like water to the sea.

In this third piece, then, the emphasis is shifting from psychology and philosophy to the Word of God. Indeed, it is not as if psychology and philosophy are "transitional" subjects and are superseded by the Word of God; rather, psychology and philosophy are expressions of the human being in their own right. Nevertheless, listening to the Word of God brings about a new "moment" in the search for the self; and, therefore, both psychology and philosophy can contribute their own expression of this new "moment" in the unfolding of the social self.

The "Word of God", then, is a part of the "intra-personal" dialogue with ourselves and God; it is, as it were, the bearer of that "confessional" truth which brings us home to ourselves. I can remember, for example, listening to the parable of the King and his invited guests, one of whom came to the wedding without a wedding garment (cf. Mt 22: 1-14), and "discovering" myself in this Gospel; and, in retrospect, I was like a man who, when it rained, did not gather water to drink but went on being thirsty. There is nothing automatic, then, about "drinking a word" that sobers us up: that communicates who we are in a way that begets a real relationship to God and to each other. Indeed, it might be said, there are many intoxicating expressions of ourselves, from being a musician to being a sculptor, artist, furniture maker, teacher, discoverer and even a writer, all of which can emphasise our own identity as if it is a project of self-construction: a kind of "identity-kit" process of self-identification. This is not to deny the reality of finding the path to ourselves through a true talent and not because of a falsification of who we are on the basis of "imitating" another because, as it were, we do not know what we are like and what will bring us "home" to ourselves.

The "Word of God", then, is very different in that it is like a dissolving cream that both takes away what does not belong to us and, at the same time, reveals the possibility of really knowing who we are. It is a "mercy" to be spoken to by this "Word" and to be "opened" to a beginning that leads to life.

A TRILOGY IN SEARCH OF SELF (III)
WATER FROM THE ROCK

The Word of God
is a mirror in which we can wash:

A deep well in which clear springs the truth.

Why dig it?

If not driven by the scent of streams
which twitched in the root of thirst.

Scripture
is a close grained Word in which lives
are layered down generations
cabling between us

hacked up unproductively –

or blasting by design
a needle of light
in a sparkless white-blue silence
in which God in Act
is at work.

A Word of life illumines life
like water on the rolled rock,
oiled in the Spirit through which
the writer writes
what is read.

Long have I searched
for the face in the facts:

a form by which to grasp
an opening out to the end.
Wisdom is the breath of God (cf. Wis 7: 25).
Hers is the hand
whose touch cracks the mud

shells the sin

and sharpens into speech
the charred song:

Glory be to the Father of
Christ the Word
whom wisdom
Loves to bear in us.

Although the water diviner, with his stick in search of water, is a relatively simple combination of sensitivity and a stick, the "twitch of life" shows itself in many different ways. In other words, whether it is a print, a painting, an idea, an "imaged" moment, a word in the Scriptures, in philosophy or in conversation, it does not matter; it is, rather, as if it is in the very nature of life "to twitch" even when it seems impossible to find water, which always finds the lowest level and leads down to the sea. Perhaps, given the desperation there may well be of searching for water when really thirsty, the "twitch of life" may be more like the residual sign of life when it is, as it were, flickering "on" and "off" as a person slips into a depressive spiralling which ends in the grave; and, therefore, this intermittent sense of purpose may be more like finding clues, when clueless about the meaning and purpose of life, which are about keeping us in the search until we are found.

WHY DID I LOOK?

late at night,
into a face on a shroud that looked like His,
when the television dot,
like a tube withdrawn,
opened a hole out of which slopped words?

Why did I announce His glory in the heat,
hidden in the roaring distance in which I tractor worked?

What origin was there to the loathing,
in between waking and sleeping,
like waste on the water's edge,
as I slipped on the slopey blackness beneath the
noble, gold-bright fortress on the hill?

Why, friendless, weeping, wounded on the phone,
did I hopeless,
hope in going home?

What awoke fear of His judgement when,
at the end of a tired-long day,
I tried to sleep into death?

Who lit the leaf,
left the pattern in natural forms,
and opened the spousal nature of reason?

Who came as a shepherd in my broken darkness?

From where came the help to think truth-fashioned thoughts
I doubted to be true,
to see, imprisoned in a hospital,
the possibility of freedom from a routine less day
and the dietary door to breathing out
of a life-time's smothering tiredness?

Why did His death
– the opening of His side –
visit me when the mother of our child said
she had aborted it?

Why did I want to be in a church,
on the sanctuary?

Why did I find,
in the opening of a woman-friend's arms,
the possibility of the same pain again?

Why did I come to hear that I am enslaved to sin;
and if enslaved – Who will make their Exodus mine?

God came to me in person,
in the person of many people,
in the person of His Son;

Love is the person (cf. 1 Jn 4-8) who stands
in my life like the cross stood in His,
until I plunge into an eternity
chosen in Him

or separated out from Him?

The same question as expressed in the last piece is now found in "Dew": if what exists did not originate with me then where did it come from? But it is not as if there is only one kind of intimation, insight, moment of beauty or thought about patterns or pieces of an answer to life's questions and, somehow, they coalesce; but, also, like water, they can evaporate, leaving "unfinished" the whole message to be communicated: a kind of "un-grasped" dialogue that, nevertheless, somehow lingers to be re-read and recognised for what it is. My response, then, was like writing in the sand when the tide was coming in and bears, as it were, the very vulnerability of an "almost" prayer.

At the same time there is a need to speak and to be heard and, in its own way, this piece intones the theme of loneliness again: a double loneliness. There is not only a human loneliness in terms of company but another kind of loneliness: a kind of "praying-less" loneliness. Did I even get as far as the question of the existence of God? It is as if a part of the poem is about not getting to the top of the mountain and looking into the windowed sky.

In another way, it is also about not having expressed what needs to be expressed in the pain of events and a life empty of company and all the frustrations of sharing and discovering that are "defined" in the very state of loneliness. In other words, we need to be heard as well as we need to be listening; and, if we do neither, there is a kind withering in the waiting for both.

DEW

Did I make the deeply dug
golden fragments
which, disturbed, I mislaid?

Did I fashion
the gem studded rose
flowering in the sparkling cold?

Did I spread out the ice-bright
cloud-scaped morn
or pour the breaking sun
upon the passing clouds?,

pausing them awhile
until the slow changes slip,

indistinguishably,
like silvery shapes into gently rocking water

and the blasting sky
dies down behind
the blackened horse
upon the brow,

leaving memories
to be drawn in the running down words
of condensating pain

melting, like snow,
suddenly starting, irregularly away down,
to the pool in the glass.

When no one is here to share
the setting of the day, it dies,
a dough baked bread

written to be shared between two
in the edible dead page
read to life again

by the silence in the other
whose waiting in the listening
is like looking
for their own route to the common ground.

If a tear does not drain
the heart does not grow.

I worked and found
a piece in different places
of a pattern in the reason
right, as always, in the blood of things.

But why a form
in the earth if the Maker
is not mirrored in the made?

The sun in the sea
drops light in my eyes,
administering beauty,

and opens, in them,
the glory edged dawn-bead-bedecked ducks
on the lake of an everyday winter's morning –

not manufactured: but as if a glistening sorrow
had set itself to rouse anew another day.

LEAVES: ALIVE AND DEAD[10]

There are many more dramatic images that could have been chosen to open this section on the experience of "Pain and Joy". But shocks, like the touch of static on a car door, are almost a part of daily life; but, at the same time, there are deeper, more tragic wounds which occur and perhaps it is necessary to go gently into that place. It may be that there is a kind of fragment of the original experience still "alive", as it were, in the memory and it is all too easy to induce a relapse of what we went through; but, nevertheless, there is a necessary cleansing of the wound and, if it is possible, to be part of a grace-prepared preparation for healing. I hope, therefore, this more organic image will still allow us to pass to what needs help without hindering us as if we were caught on a wire fence, a bramble or a ragged edge – to pass to hope and to what is yet to come.

---

[10] Copyright permission given by email, 1/5/2019: Credit G D Bebeau; and the collection from which it came can be found at: https://www.friendsofthewildflowergarden.org/pages/plants/labradorte a.html.

PART IV

PAIN AND JOY

An Unexpected Joy: An Unprecedented Pain

Sin does not describe the experience of suddenly, unexpectedly, discovering an inexplicable joy that arises out of the conception of a child; indeed, however aware we were of the possibility of conceiving a child, there came an unforgettable joy from the very roots of human being. Whatever the "noisy" claims about a "clump of cells" - the reality of parenthood had an unmistakable beginning: a trumpeting joy. It is possible to understand human psychology as if our whole being is a kind of self-originating expression of conscious reactions; however, given that the very existence of each one of us arises out of relationships, it is not possible to understand ourselves except "through" relationship. Perhaps we need to recognise, then, that seeing is seeing something or someone: that there is a kind of interior dialogue between ourselves and what exists. Consciousness is not just about "admitting" the presence of a self – it is also about dialoguing with what is real. Thus, on reflection, the joy that arose was as indistinguishable from the very coming into existence of "another" as it was unbidden; indeed, as surrounded as this moment was by all kinds of difficulties and uncertainties, it is extraordinary that it was joy that rang out.

Joy and pain express "relationship"

But then the child was aborted. Whatever was half-thought about the existence of a beginning, an initial moment of animation, the various possibilities of our lives, the pain of discovering that that child's life had been abruptly, terribly ended, was a pain as uninvited and prolonged as the joy had been brief and brilliant. Thirty years on, however, this child is as present to me as every other child; and, even if I cannot explain it, I am conscious of a fatherhood that I cannot forget. Just as children are constantly around me, as I am now married and my wife and I have ten children, two of whom miscarried and we hope are also in heaven, so this child of thirty years ago is as present to me as they all are. Even if one is away from the dining room table, whether just briefly for a party elsewhere, an outing or for a longer expedition, it is not possible to describe, adequately, the "silence" of the children's absence. Thus this child of thirty years is still present in "his" absence in a way that makes a lie of every account that denies the reality of both the unborn and the relationship which comes into existence with the very beginning of each child.

Recognising an unborn child is about recognizing the "reality" of relationship

Whether a child is lost through a miscarriage or an abortion, never mind the many other possibilities that can bring about such a loss, there is an inseparable relationship which has come to exist and which continues, unabated, to call for development; indeed, as difficult as it is to understand, a relationship can undergo all kinds of changes even through the mystery of death. To begin with, there is seeking forgiveness and asking for help; indeed, Charlie's abortion, while an indelible experience, did not of itself make me chaste. The pain, however, made me conscious of another relationship: the relationship of mother and child – the relationship of the Mother of God and her son Jesus Christ. As what Mother Teresa would call a 'broken Christian', I vacillated between going to Church and living a life that expressed an inability to commit myself to anyone or anything. Nevertheless, in that "moment" of grief, I was vividly conscious of the dead Christ in the arms of His Mother; and, at the same time, the unavoidable consciousness of the painful death of the innocent: the innocence of Christ and the innocence of Charlie. If it can be called a consolation – although it is scarcely possible to experience the comfort of that consolation, so painful is the realisation of participation, however inadvertent and unintended, in the event of abortion – then it was as if the Mother of the Lord communicated the mystery of salvation: that just as the death of her own Son was not in vain, neither was the death of this child in vain. Indeed, if the loss of one child can cause so much pain, how much unacknowledged suffering must exist because of the daily denial of human fatherhood?

What about, too, the discovery that anyone who has "given" a part of what constitutes the mystery of life to another or to an experiment has given a relationship of life to life, of one person to another, that is as real as the living being that has come into existence? We live in a culture, then, that at some time will discover – or become more dreadful in its denial – that we live amidst a multitude of relationships that it may take our entry into eternity to actually admit, acknowledge and address as the real effect of our actions.

Religious experience and pain are not conversion

Pain discloses all kinds of regret and impoverishment, from an uncertainty about vocation, abilities and training to the intricate, difficult and challenging depths that are at work in our lives. In other words, even if these experiences began to make it clear that I could not marry because I did not have faith, they neither made it clear what faith was nor how to come to it; indeed, I can remember thinking that I could not marry because I did not have the faith to endure the inescapable sufferings of marriage – yet I could not have told you what it was about faith that made it possible to endure the sufferings of marriage. Clearly, however, there was some nascent awareness that faith makes possible endurance. Thus, by default, as it were, I discovered that I neither had faith nor knew what it was. But, at the same time as my life showed more and more clearly the devastation wrought from within, I was almost involuntarily incapable of finding truth to be a sufficient answer to the disorder which was increasingly evident. I could recognise, for example, that for years I had been seeking to find a path to employment: a path which both identified a particular, "workable talent" and, at the same time, the number of different routes that I chose to pursue argued, cumulatively, for the realisation that I did not know who I was. I did not seem to possess a stable identity. I was neither married nor single, neither priest nor monk, neither writer nor painter, neither sculptor nor craftsman, although I had "passed through" the possibility of being all of them and had ended up as none of them.

Self-discovery is not the same as being discovered by God

Certain insights are, as it were, like the rediscovery of the human being: that each human person is essentially relational: that the human person is constituted by origin, relationship and identity: that each person is both an originator and a recipient of relationships. But we originate relationships, not because we brought ourselves into existence, but because we were "caused" to exist: we were loved into existence. Love, in a sense, is nothing if not relational; it is impossible to love if there is no one to love. The point, then, of this is that there are many invaluable insights about the heart of human personhood which arise, inciden-tally, in the course of truly seeking to bring about a whole human existence: an answer to the pain of not knowing exactly who we are and the purpose of life.

Not only, then, is relationship the dynamic vehicle of self-development; but, in a sense, the refusal of relationship is at the root of psychological problems. I recall, for instance, being unable and indeed "unwilling" to admit the pain of humiliations that I experienced as a school child; and, as a result, I "throttled" the whole, human reaction, which would have disclosed the interior of my childhood. It was not until much later, then, that I rediscovered the experience that had once been a part of my "present". The "living memory" had "remained" but had been inaccessible until a "dam" broke and I became conscious of streaming memories, unabated, as if like compost it cannot become a part of the ground out of which comes growth until it has more naturally "soaked" in and through consciousness. The thought, then, that arises from the material of our experience, needs that experience to be available in the kind of way that voluntary recall makes possible; but if, for whatever reason, pride speaks through the unwillingness to admit sufferings, then not only does pride itself remain hidden but so, too, do the dynamics of development which depend on self-disclosure.

The recovery of personal history, however, is not the same as recognising the history of salvation; and, while philosophical naturalism has immense merits, it is not the same as discovering ourselves in the action of God. Thus discovering our foundational relationship to God is essential, not just to the truth of life but to conversion: that just as God created all that exists from nothing so He can make a new beginning for the sinner (cf. *Catechism of the Catholic Church*, paragraph 298). In the prose-poem which follows there is a brief account of the pain and joy of becoming a father and then losing the child to abortion.

INDELIBLE

Joy announced you to me.

I know the smothering imperfection of our time:
the anxious lying of single people –
am I a father? am I a mother?
do we have a child?

"Your" existence your mother denied:
her lie to my uncertainty, a slipperiness supplied –

and my heart filled,
as I foresaw her,
beside me,
stretching out our tent:
swelling,
growing rounder

and my hands and body knowing
life between us growing
from within us both beginning
but now in her becoming -

And again I pulled apart:

"Are we married?
Have we the right?
To love as lovers and unite?"

But then I saw, as in a sleepless dream,
in an in-hospitable place, being done what we cannot undo:

separating what God had joined together.

Your mother and I met again,
and her secret, she shared:

That she thought you were a "blobby mass";
and, because of it,

You are no longer where you were.

Listening was a splashing pain,
a splintering, swiftly slicing pain.

"I'm sorry" was a word too heavily burdened to be spoken.

We named and prayed for you.

Too personal, I know, to make public, but public it now is,
because too many died, before you,
and you did to me what millions did not do.

I was wrong, I know, to love when love was not
committed, between your mother and me.

Listening was a splashing pain,
a splintering, swiftly lashing pain.

And I pulled apart again - hurting hard again:

a hidden shard of pain,
seizing leaving as a means
to hurt her hard again.
.
"I am sorry": a word that grew in me to speak.

Listening was a splashing pain,
a splintering, swiftly swiping pain.
"I am sorry" is a word to strengthen the weak.

Reconciled
Your mother and I parted.

The dead Christ-child lay in the arms of Mary:
a blooming brightening
unforgettable being.
And out of Love's many-chambered-petalled-heart,
our child spoke like scent:

"Look and see the Crucified:
His Resurrection is our new life.
Do not escape your suffering and
it will give you life again.

When Easter crowns the crucifixion and
completes the gift of Christmas –
we will go up in song,
and love will cry out:
Amen in song!
Amen in sight!
Amen!

When I hear of people locked into the desire for death, I remember the times of turning to suicide and want to light a burning love and drop a hope-ladder into the person's pit. There is a kind of impenetrable meaningless, perhaps even a cyclical decline, like a drill turning down more deeply each time into the earth and, at the same time, water running into the bottom of the hole and making everything wet, cold and sludgy. In other words, help has to come from another. We cannot "lift" ourselves out of the grinding down grime. Boredom is a part of it in the sense of undiscovered interests which, being "un-visible" are not there to bring friendships with them or acquaintances never become friends because of the unexpressed life that is like an all but stifled flame: stifling both the person almost completely silent and the communication that belongs to companionship.

Thus this next piece is a "passing" into that place, those times, in which meaning eludes our life like oxygen being siphoned from a room; and, in that "moment" of the asphyxiation of meaning, I beg you to read this poem. I want you to discover or uncover the lie in the temptation to give up on searching out the significance in the facts of life.

SUICIDE

comes upon us slowly,
like the death of a tree
or car fume poisoning,
a growing opaqueness,
a dripping drowning
or a trailing away
into a "non-returnable" silence.

Nobody knows why this is the "moment";
having run away and returned,

already there is a suffocating suffering:

suffocation
takes time but collapses to an end:

erosion cavities the earth,
land swamps and
fires burn down.

It is night,
a quiet intensity,

passing thoughts about being missed,

a little room, a bottle of pills and water.

Time shrinks to a droplet before evaporation,
when an unbidden image of
Christ the Judge and His disciples unexpectedly
makes me question what I am doing and,
sweating,

I drink lots of water.

Silence enclosed this moment,
like many others,
lying in the life-past,
now uncovered,
undergoing decomposition or returning in the present?

Exploring that moment
is like trying to climb into a small "space",
too shrunk to be easily "opened"

needing empathy
to expand the heart to embrace the painful joy of
being alive.

Sometimes the search within is a description of a hidden life; and, in describing it, a communicating of the "inside pain": to be with it in a way that is not about altering it. Indeed, in human terms, I doubt if we can really alter what comes to be internally; and, in that sense, our words are more like a message in "space": an "un-knowing" if it helps to have "voiced-a-word".

It is not as if we deliberately choose the internal conse-quences of our actions so much as we refuse the process of being humbled in the course of admitting our sufferings. Thus "Hidden" is about that sense of what happened, within, in refusing to admit the pain of childhood humiliations: of being ridiculed and caned for failing to understand studying.

There is, however, a kind of "intuition" about the help of Christ. Even if it is not clear to me when this was written or how convinced of it I was, I think it is a bit like knowing that He has helped others and that it is possible for Him to help me. At the same time there is a sense that the sufferings are "impossible" and beyond, as it were, psychological help, although healing has to entail the psychological interior of a person's life; and, indeed, I can remember a time "of remem-bering": a time when what had been "un-remembered" was suddenly free to be remembered, like the breaking of a dam. Nevertheless the appeal to Christ "within" the suffering indicates that there was a "scent" of purpose, even if it was still to be discovered more fully; and, furthermore, that there is a healing of pride which is a work of the word of God and, although beyond the reach of psychological help, is nevertheless expressed psychologically in the willingness to be of service to others.

HIDDEN

My face melted inwards and clogged up speech.

Tears burnt down the growing tip and glazed it.

Who can open the glass eye?

Who can grow the dead end?

Who can un-confuse the congealed heart
and draw the pussed ugliness
on which it is impaled?

Christ,
hidden in His-our suffering
bleeds life into us.

The next one was written in the Light of Christmas, December 1994, while attending a Job Club in the hope of finding work or a course to further my prospects of work. It was one of many occasions of various durations of unemployment as, indeed, I had not yet finished my first degree, which was in theology, and I had only been published occasionally, being paid even more occasionally. Work was very intermittent and it was a struggle to come from a failed schooling into office work, a "no man's land", forays into artistic and literary interests, failing at university, into a practical line of work and then into a different, more literary or learned type of work; and, at thirty eight, there was still no definite direction or pattern to my life but only an impossible to relinquish quest to research, to write and persevere in the impossible hope of being published and paid. Indeed, what hopes I had of being a writer were scarcely imaginable or sustainable, except in so far as writing was generally a part of the studying that I did, which proved to be the beginning of a focus of qualifications which, however, were not to bear fruit in employment until over a decade later.

In many ways this is a part of the difficulty of a "criss-cross crisis" in the search for work, talents and vocation. Indeed, crossing from one kind or type of work to another was almost constantly arresting the progress it meant to be because it was like continually going back to the beginning and not getting beyond the initial engagement with a subject or type of work.

In general, however, the passing of these years was a round of humbling visits to job centres, interviews, courses, rejection slips and inconclusive outcomes, not to mention course failures and temporary positions or types of self-employment that went nowhere or in a direction that I did not, in end, want or was capable of going in.

THE PRAYER IN OUR SEARCH FOR WORK

BREAD FOR THE BROKEN, WINE FOR THE UNWANTED

You and I are a gift:
a gift formed in the family
and given in friendship.

Let our hearts grow
in the body of our home.

But if frustration, anger, disappointment and even
injustice, discourage us; if uncertainty,
fear, failure and illness undermine us; and if poverty,
debt, depression, unhappiness and loneliness
turn us to temptation; and
If we cannot overcome our unwillingness to believe that God is
love (1 Jn 4: 8), or even that He exists –

Let us beg God to crack open
our hope in this dried out
seed-cased opportunity of unemployment:

Let us sow a seed in this darkness
and light a prayer:

O God, to this gift of ourselves,
wed the willingness to believe
that nothing is impossible to you (cf. Lk 1: 37).

It is as if whatever remnant of the fairy tale "gloss" on life
was stripped off in a single, bleaching glance; and, in that

moment, the stress of shopping with three young children completely disappeared.

There was nothing – except there was a real peace and the coming back of the child called back from being led away by a stranger – and then she was there again. Although the police said this area was rarely a cause of this kind of concern it may be more because these "almost disappearances" came to nothing. Again, this time on the roadside, a driver going the opposite way to our son coming home, stopped and asked him to get in – but then drove off as he ran home; and, again, the police seemed to think this was a rare occurrence and needed more reports to be taken further – but not, we hope, the reports of children having disappeared and remaining un-found.

So there is the difficulty of describing the pain of passing, however briefly, through the uncertainty of losing a child. At the same time, there are those who have lost their children, wives, husbands and who live, day by day, whatever tormented hope of their return. How many different pains there are that arise out of our relationships among one another? It is almost as if the "passing of pain" is a part of the pulse which beats between us: an unbearable pulse that needs relief and healing help. There are times when, from the sheer grief of life, it would be easier to die than to take another pulse of that pain; and then, in the unexpected moment of change, the irreplaceable tears of how beautifully true that I have lived long enough to know the day to day love of an everyday dad.

LOSING HER

however briefly,
to the stealing hand of another.

In that moment of standing still,
she is nowhere to be seen,
seconds out of sight around the flower stall,
she is indescribably gone:
a kind of glowing absence as if she is still there
but I cannot see her anywhere.

Instead of panic and exploring everywhere,
imagining how to rush about with two children still beside me,
a full trolley and where to begin and to whom to turn
a prayer prompts me
to look towards the check-out
and there she is,
led by another hand
towards who knows where.

First a fruitlessly nervous first call,
barely audible,
and then a second,
louder,
more blasting naming of my child
which unlocks the hand
leading her away
to let her return and stay.

I cannot tell you how many times I have thanked You
that in the moment of her absence I prayed
and saw her leaving
suffering,
afterwards,
the replay

of other possibilities
and the scars of fear and
sickening helplessness
in front of
almost
losing her

but now knowing that
she is growing into life!

There are many, too numerous challenges to our humanity, which threaten to turn the goals of mankind into self-destructive extinguishing of others: abortion; human embryo experimentation; organ stripping of prisoners[11]; human trafficking and exploitation of the poor; indeed, self-destructive acts disfigure our identity, our relationships, our culture, our ecological home and our consciences.

At the same time, however, the heart has to be touched at a particular place and, like the spreading of warmth, it has to go through us to others; and, therefore, once begun, there is a borderless expanse of interconnected sufferings: a possibility of either a despairing paralysis or a prayerful going into the mystery of human misery. Through the "glitz" of success, whether scientific, artistic or commercial, there is often a "space" which opens on a person or a people's plight to be revealed; and, in the exploration of that plight, there arises the enriching concern and the compelling account of the complexities of that suffering. Perhaps, even, there is an unexpected beauty, like the water which brings out the colour in pebbles; and, little by little, there is a subtly morphing

---

[11] Cf. Peter Chojnowski, Ph.D: "Red Harvest: China's Prisoner Organ Trafficking Attacked at Vatican Conference":
http://www.cmq.org.uk/CMQ/2017/Nov/china-organ-traficking2.html.

awareness of the need to step through the refracting images and help.

"Freezing", then, is one of those points of contact with our humanity which, like frostbite, risks scaring us into withdrawal; or, alternatively, it sends us reeling to the conclusion that there is a wealth of contributions to be made to the humanisation of mankind. Day by day there needs to be a kind of global holding hands, hand by hand, as we shed the isolation which allowed the pitiless gaze to seize another. In time, there will be dancing as another hand is held; and then mourning, as another heart is lost. Thus this piece turns to another of the needs to turn our hoping into helping and our helping into hoping to be in time.

FREEZING

is indescribably stopping a beginning:
a beginning begun in the outward mixing of what
God personalised through recognising
His own work in the unnatural handling of human "potters".

The outward cold of freezing a begun beginning
communicates an inward cold blowing through the scientific
possibilities stripped of perception: of perceiving
the living being blurred
through research methods and techniques
that turn the living into tools of enquiry.

What warmth there may have been in the general hope of helping
mankind is now generating below zero temperatures:
a manufactured stillness
that steals the pulse of change.

Just as a snowflake[12] is
fragility itself,
delicately beautiful,
and typically unique

So are you!
If you could voice waiting to be delivered
from gassing ice ...

If you could speak of being an investigation that took the gift of life
...
If you could cry out of the contradiction
of being equally given the gift of life
but then of it being unequally taken ...
What wonder to be discovered will rediscover

---

[12] Cf. Jamie Dean, "Hope for the unchosen",
https://world.wng.org/2018/01/hope_for_the_unchosen.

the wonder of beholding
the gifts of understanding
integral
to giving back
what we freely received?

We simply grow: an unfolding of "who" began in love's entailing
embrace.

Wherefrom comes the thaw that humanises cross-currents,
harnessing humanity's hope of helping us all?

What morphing of "slavery and exploitation"
will morph into service:

simple or sophisticated healing
of ambitious plans into
concrete works of mercy?

Are we equally gift or unequally product?

We live in a society wounded beyond human strength to
heal and yet, in the mystery of forgiveness, there is an answer
beyond death to the myriad difficulties that drive, death upon
death, down into the depths of our being.

Within each of us and each of our families there are those
experiences, however brief, that begin the splitting down of
what unites us. Whether it is a scathing word that feeds on a
dissatisfaction and the fantasy of finding happiness with
another or the hurt that turns us to seek how to hurt back or
the daily difficulties that bleed our patience until we are raw
and want to run away, we need the help of Love in us loving to
love even when love is dying in the daily defeat of the person
we thought we were and cry out to be.

THE FAMILY TREE

If we split apart:
are driven down
in weeping pieces –
then who will find
the tree in splintered trunk
and flailing offspring?

Only each of us
bound
in the arms of Christ.

TRAVELLING[13]

This picture takes us into the theme of "Passing Through" as, quite literally, it is a picture that involves the double imagery of travelling, of passing through a variety of places, and yet it also includes a young man sitting opposite a woman and the whole tension of being inattentive to the other while apparently absorbed in using a phone. In terms of the real situation it maybe that the young man has a good reason to be on his phone; but, in terms of using this picture and giving it the context of this part of the book, it is possible to "read" the situation as a kind of social loneliness: of being present to another but of hiding the desire to communicate – either behind a phone or a book or a general denial of seeking to go beyond the isolation of always passing through people's lives.

---

[13] The picture was published by Victoriano Izquierdo on a free to use website called: https://unsplash.com/photos/VGOiY1gZZYg.

PART V

PASSING THROUGH

Loving, being in love, falling in love, there are so many expressions for what, really, often "passes" for love; indeed, it is not that we have necessarily lied so much as we have been incapable of understanding what love is or even actually loving. There is no doubt that people are drawn to each other for a variety of reasons; and, paradoxically, perhaps one of those reasons is the "absence" of reason. In other words, perhaps loving is not so much "turning" to another as "turning" away from a self: as if loving is like hiding from a pain that hides in the company of others. This is not so much a deliberate strategy as a kind of "absorption-in-passing": as if we are passing into company like shadows crossing in the street; indeed, being undeveloped and not knowing what life is about is like being collapsed and needing activity like a balloon needs inflating. The purpose of a day can be measured between the time together and the time to come together again; and, in between, there can be all kinds of "filler" activities, whether going to the library, trying to study, writing, going to the doctor or giving up and going back to the "bed-sitting-waiting room".

Over many years and in a variety of ways there has been a growing towards others: an "other"; and, in a certain way, perhaps this is a kind of relational apprenticeship: a kind "trial and error" in the field of meeting others. But, nevertheless, this is a very grubby activity and, at times, there is a kind of sickening in front of the mess of disappointing failures, premature advances and a kind of churning over what went wrong and the interminable questioning of motives and actions. Without, then, there being a kind of obvious progress, these "poems" are about "passing through" relationships in a way that destroys a simple optimism that the next one will work out, be better or lead to the hope for happiness. Elsewhere I have written of the gift of faith that made marriage possible; here, in some of its pitiable characteristics, are a variety of accounts through which I stumbled and fell and, towards the end, an intimation of a newness not my own.

In "Psalm 151", having failed to find love, there is a turning towards the possibility that it is impossible to find it for myself; and, in that coldness 'of parting in the sea' there is a "prayer-gap" arising out of yet another failure to find happiness. Or rather, failing to love is sickening into disappointment: a bitter-sweet tasting of forbidden fruit that turns sour in the aftermath. The meaning of life unravels an emptiness that never really filled and spurs another foray into friendship without really getting any closer to the needs of the heart for healing.

PSALM 151

I do not want to want what is not:

the gardens, the museums, the walks upon the beach;
the shopping, and quarrelling, holding onto each;
the noise of what we do, and eat and speech;

and how I held you, and how you loved me to,
making up the bliss it was, the kiss it was.

But what freedom have I from the promise of the past:
when your absence was a presence;
and I lived the week on what had and was to pass?

I want to feel the cold of parting in the sea:
the sheering separation of becoming you and me.

I want the word that you have since wed
to weld a silence in my soul,
where what is dying will die
and what is living will not again
be wanted in the loss.

Oh living God:
- give me again the love of living I have lost;
- bring me good news, I pray, of how to love and
love not to betray;
- bring me good news, I pray, of one who loves me, and
will love me, day after endless day.

Is loneliness like the "isolation" of the drops of a wave: a reality as temporary as the fall of far flung water until, plunging afresh into the sea, they recover their place in the whole? As a young man discovering how ruptured his capacity for friendship was, the loneliness did not seem like the scattering of isolated drops, which were once part of a wave; rather, the loneliness seemed like an endless emptiness, going nowhere, just getting worse and more and more conspicuous. The pain of standing on a dance floor, unable to come out of the self-consciousness of "being alone", driving me out of the pub and back to the lonely walks, did not seem like a temporary "moment" but more like a "life sentence" – a great neon sign pointing to myself-on-my-own in an unbearable way.

How to convey, in a relatively few words, the years of bed-sits, sharing that was more selfish than caring, unsuccessful solitude, the vulnerability to self-pity and the inability to pass to the "other" and to help someone else?

LONELINESS

is an island on a mountainous foundation.

Before the me I can be
was open to the "we" I am –

the sparkling sea ebbed away
and spread out its draining word:

lie in my bottomless hands.

Why did I walk on past
the sea's edging entrance?

Why not drop into the cold ocean,
parting what leaves no trace of being parted?

Why did I walk on past
the splintering-smashed-splash
as it swept up, sprayed out,
abandoned to the sky –

to fall –

in drops where once it was a wave?

The unbearably empty beach,
cold and warmthless,

grey skies and hard, relentless rock, resisting the bashing of the
waves – but breaking, all the same,
on a single person out of his depth.

Bedsits, although furnished,
occasionally visited,
were a refuge for refusing
to recognise the "problems of life" they expressed
or concealed.

Was the prayer of my father heard?
Or the tears of my mother answered?

What day-break
broke unseen
and bled a promise in my died out heart?

Loneliness is a lie being uncovered:
a hissing pain in a kissing touch –

Believe you are loved!

I can almost remember the "moment" of 'glistening' mud
and wonder, nevertheless, at the human, personal context of
the whole piece. What strikes me now, then, is the eruption of
'a wail ... between us' and the possibility of either death or
parting or even a mixture of both bringing this about. In other
words, there are times when the too beautiful splendour of
nature is like a poignant reminder of a picked rose: a flowered
meeting that, being uprooted, slowly withered and had to be
thrown away. Or maybe it was the memory of a death
returning, like a lingering sadness, to steal away what would
have otherwise been a wonderful moment. Either way, we
need both beauty and the pain we experience to help each
other.

MUD

mounds bound the meandering river:

damp, lumpy, black jewelled dough, sprinkled with glistening
in the afternoon silence of a blessing in the day.

A sun-smiling swept across the bright white wet
and a wail arose between us.

The bare tree,
a full darkness against the night sky,
stretched out skyward
against the mauve-blue-pink-lilac like evening pointillism.

Death, an embrace between outstretched hearts of opened,
emptied love, filled fully and made fast,
death like this is life:

crying out to be taken in with everything that God called out
in giving us life!

Grief and gratitude,
if alone are extremes apart but,
together, mix and mellow one another,
mending in the tempering,
one of the other,
the wounded
weakened heart.

In what follows, it is as if in the very experience of
conscience there is a far more active dialogue than we
generally realise; indeed, a dialogue that makes the one who
argues with us, in our heart, "The Friend" that makes
friendship possible.

THE FRIEND

When the day is done
and words come when there were none
and we, arm in arm now breast on chest
come closer, closer come.

Then came a friend between us,
came dancing like a flame,
burning what was melting
and parting us again.

Our kiss was like desertion
but He fought against our flight:
are you married? have you the right?
to love as lovers and unite.

And when we pulled apart
and tore at each other's heart
there formed,
forgiveness,

Like a friend fulfilled in us
the promise of His faithfulness.

There are times and places when we think beauty is pulsing through the place we are; but, in reality, it is a place beyond the place it is. But, in retrospect, it is as if there is a passing of a beckoning beauty that is calling us through the moment to be beyond where we are. Like a current in the sea that ebbs and flows until, frightened though we were, we are beached in a place we would not have found but for the pulsing path that brought us there. The moment, however, of encountering happiness, however briefly, has a kind of magnetic fastness and, almost like the limpet on the rock, makes us cling to what we cannot hold on to and thus risk drowning in the sea of difficulties which surround the "un-anchored".

IN THE CHURCH WOOD

the many green leaves run along their
dark meshed veins and flicker in the breeze.

The breathing green blaze,
sweeping through the scene,
blows bright and pale again.

Blue and white sky-stars,
like scattered brightnesses,
are in-breaking the leafy twigged tightness.

The breathing green blaze,
sweeping through the scene,
blows bright and pale again.

The ever-never-stopping-streaming-stream
runs polluted where it stood its ground in times
past and present and presently ongoing.

Can the running water run back to the beginning
and break afresh the brooked freshness?

If a worm is in the wood
will the *Bird of God* seize it dead?

The breathing green blaze,
sweeping through the scene,
blows bright and pale again.

When the light passes into action
then will the waves mount up
into pulsed grained grace
and grow out the dying
done without it.

Weariness of life is not just a want or exhaustion of energy, a temporary reading of "below empty", pulling at the roots of our strength and craving a respite, however temporary, from the demands of the day; rather, it is an erosion of hope, corroded out of us like failure and rejection sap the very will to live and the possibility of "bouncing back" breaks, as it were, with the growing inflexibility that comes with bitterness and disappointment. But to see this, this is the grace: that day in day out we live on an expectation of happiness that is like the froth on a drink, lacking substance and sustenance and covering, in its way, the drugging of sensibility and reason; and yet, compulsively, we get up and lunge from one relationship to another, hoping it will be different or not even consciously caring but, like alcoholics, seeking the next oblivion. But not even consciously seeking another immersion in what obstructs thought and reflection and the radical realisation that there is a decline in the steps forward that is really taking us down to where we do not really want to go.

EXPERIENCE

in my experience repeats itself.

My experience of remaining unmarried continues to carry
down replicating chains of months and years and tears,
locked in an en-cloning
multiplication of repetition.

What hooks the eye repeatedly but releases pain instead of
pleasure?

A hidden-in sin?
A secret sunk-fast but showing in the devastation?
Will Christ denature this virulent vice?
and turn me out
to be free to marry?

For if now I can see-hear
the clinks down the years
it is from the grace within reason,
an in-searing instruction,

a cause in the falling
through pain
to an alms-fast-prayer

attacking the knots in a cord
that shorten a life
lived without the wheel
turning conversion,

like a walk in the rain
is rinsing off the claim
of an addictive habit
it was wrong to maintain.

Bless God in this
time it is His to provide
the word to divide

me from the hell inside,
leaving a hope in the sign
of an unfinished sentence:

"completed in LIFE".

In the last three poems of this part of the collection, there is a temptation to think of an apprentice's progress as a kind of learning through suffering in the discovering of failing in love; however, this is called a temptation because, in my experience, we need more than the melting of optimistic hopes and the arising, yet again, of that "unfounded expectation" that it is possible to begin again.

The first piece, then, is called "Grape-Juice" and recalls a moment of an almost promised friendship, 'Out splashed a bright love' which, in the third piece of this trilogy, is more explicitly stated: 'I judged by appearances and missed the opportunity of meeting one who wanted to meet me.' I recall, then, being in a library and wondering about how to talk to a girl in my class who was also there, who then tells me about another girl who "liked me". In other words, while I am still trying to find words to speak to the girl in front of me, she tells me of another. This "possible" encounter became a real snare of thoughts along the lines of "if only"; but then the whole history of failed and failing relationships "kicks in" and "pops" the ballooning of past possibilities.

But, moreover, it is not just about the occasional dis-appointment, as deeply disturbing as that can be, leaving an unwillingness to warm to another, lest another rejection expose the first unresolved hurt and complicate it with another; rather, it is about a dreadful course of disappointments, like falling through rapids and barely avoiding head-on collisions with rocks and then arriving, exhausted, at the bottom of this cascading calamity only to try to get up and to carry on.

A Trilogy of a Kind (I)

Grape-juice

Out
Splashed
a bright love:
a clean wound-burst
in which I saw no sin.

But bubbles burst
like wind in the bowels
from what no longer food remains.

If suffering is unacceptable
the daily bread inedible,
then either a lie threw
sunlight over everything
or his heart impaled
on the point at which
sharp shadow struck out
from strong light.

What word will slip
like a steel in the bank
and strike strength
in a mud waste running to nowhere
and stop a bog belched kiss unto death?

What will stop this
turning on a thorn?
What will answer
the questioning years
in which I neither married
nor became a priest?

What will stop this
turning through thorns
at the point of decision?

In this second piece, altogether a different mood to the last one, it is already in that season of grace which followed the gift of believing that God exists to help the sinner; and, while that is an exaggeration, it nevertheless expresses the force of change which came, unexpectedly, through being visited with faith. Thus, this second piece is written in the time of courtship and, while wistfully beginning with a sense of being outside the prospect of 'other people's happiness', yet is actually written in the time which led to my own marriage. There is no doubt, actually, that happiness had its moments and, in particular, I remember a visit from my fiancée who had come in black and pinks and indeed did look a blossoming delight. Thus, together with a chaste courtship, this period did possess its unexpected delights even if, in the context of a sapping weariness of life, deadlines, working in a laundry and other "drains" on my heart, it was almost impossible to feel the breeze and enjoy the sunshine of these days as the shadows of so many failures threatened, like a summer storm, to stifle a beautiful moment of grace.

A Trilogy of a Kind (II)

Blossom

falls and lies as if from a
wedding feast
for other people's happiness.

I must be one of the uninvited
because I do not know how to be happy.

Bitterness is a cold wind
that drives right into summer.

But I am glad of Spring:
of first opening leaves and
scent that fills the yard
behind the door.

For this beauty is not my work.

Effortlessly comes its noiseless moment
not like my every effort to make a future
that now lies nailed in the past –

and I think of what the monk said:
"What opens is a sign to the will of God."

We did not work to meet and walked out
like grains ground and watered,
flour clumping into dough.

Nor did we green the trees,
or plan the leaves
to dart almost white grey plumes,

standing out a-dripping-silvery budding
against the colding gloom.

And while we cannot rush happiness to happen,
neither let us stop, either, its glancing smile
and steady turn in the cycle of things,
turned in the hands of our gardening God.

We think of shrugging off the past or previous experiences of turmoil, indecision, "lost" or "missed" opportunities but, in reality, our lives question us relentlessly about the reasons for being the way we are or having the life we have lived; and, therefore, there is an enlightening which we need and cannot obtain for ourselves: a brightening of life which comes, in its own way, through the forgiveness of our sins and the word of God which makes a new beginning a reality and not just another possibility. Thus while we can long to be have been someone else and to have had a different history we are, in fact, the people we are precisely because of the past we have had; indeed, this tendency to look at ourselves as if we have ruined, like a frost, the fledgling tree, is all too indicative of looking without seeing the artist who is expressing a work of art in us (cf. Eph 2: 10).

Bitter experiences did focus me on a key question of what I have in common with a woman that I might marry or who might marry me: Are you open to life?; but, at the same time, learning from experience is not the same as the experience of grace: of the gift of a new beginning. We come, then, into the company of each other with the whole of what we are and what God is doing with us. I am reminded, then, that only a few months after this was written I married and the words which ran through me were: This poor man called and the Lord heard him (Ps 34: 6); and, after over twenty years of marriage, those words have not ceased to have their meaning but, rather, have grown roots in the very depths of my being. On the one hand, human experience has definitely showed me that there is an ongoing truth to my poverty before the Lord; but, in the nature of grace being freely given, it becomes a source of hope that if my poverty remains so will His help! On the other hand, in the answer of the Lord to the call of this 'poor man' is the gift of my wife. In other words, just as Adam exclaimed "This at last is bone of my bones and flesh of my flesh" (Gn 2: 23), so I can see that my wife is, as it were, chosen for me; and, therefore, all the difficulties and delights of marriage are as integral to the path through which I will come, if I come, to salvation, as the very grace of God which makes it possible.

A Trilogy of a Kind (III)

The Question

if answered
could bring me up to date
with the past:

Why was my first love
not my last?

I judged by appearances and
missed the opportunity of meeting
one who wanted to meet me.

When I was older, what did I find
But that I did not know me:

going out with a woman
was like meeting in an urgent silence,
filled awkwardly with walking
and the expectation of being interrupted
in my attempt at talking,
talking about things
that taught me I didn't know what to say.

Questioning my own silence
began a dialogue out of which
I could speak to others.

Oh how many times I tried to find someone else
while remaining hidden in myself!

How may fights have scraped
the face in me to see

I cannot expect you to be
except what in your freedom you have chosen to be!
Oh how beautiful it is to find
you have chosen what I have chosen
and that God gives us to choose
one choice between the two of us!

Learning to Type[14]

I cannot remember, exactly, where and when beginning to write took hold – but it must have been around the time I was doing a Foundation Year in Fine Art. I seem to remember that as I had started reading biographical studies in psychology, like *Dibs in Search of Self* by Virginia Axline, that I began writing a version of my own search for self. I have always regretted, however, never keeping this work; but, even so, one aspect of that time was writing with a pen on paper and the rewriting was a real problem: what was rewritten never seemed to "fit back into the text" of what had been written before. Thus I ended up with lots of sheets with Tipp-Ex, alterations, glued pieces and pages and a sense of how impossible it was to order or finish anything. This kind of intermittent writing went on for a long time until I abandoned it out of a kind of practical despair of being able to finish anything.

When I eventually went to university, and left the degree unfinished, I attended a type-writing course and began to type; and, I have to say, although it was many years before I ever owned a word-processor, my learning to type has been one of the simplest and most helpful skills I ever acquired.

---

14 Dung Anh: .https://unsplash.com/photos/AgQaMOQFWeA.

PART VI

WRITING

How much time has it taken to be writing "full-time"? A life-time of occasional pieces, growing off-line and scrapped and then, owing to the modernization of methods, accumulating files upon files of drafted work in an electronic box. Passing from the disappointment of being unpublished to the disappointment of remaining unremunerated, even when published, to beginning again, taking up additional, more media-savvy means of communication; but, at the same time, seeing whole books as "downloadables" and wondering: What happened to the author's royalties? Whose website has scraped off the meagre grain of years and years of work?

To be published, then, is like building an online library of works to be raided. Or, the alternative, to remain "shelved" on the computer until it crashes and trashes the whole lot? Better to be in print and read than dead in the box rubbished, at the end, as no one cares about that life-time's work which never paid any bills or got a "book launch" party!

Writing? What justifies it? There is the author's need to explore the myriad and challenging questions that really exist; and, at the same time, to wake up to the need of others to be able to read what helps to be written. The "outbreak of writing", as it were, cf originally coming out of an almost inexpressibly solid silence has subsided to a much more molten approach to wondering how to reach the reader as well as how to read the reality to be written about.

Writing, then, maybe more about "tuning in" to what really matters to the writer; and, although it may be possible to "try" many genres, in reality I am the writer I am and need to recognise what it is that I want to write. Thus there is the discovery of what kind of writing is more like flight that falling over. In general, then, becoming a writer may be like the coalescence of rainfall as it passes through the hillside and becomes a stream. Motives are multiple and, on the one hand, earning a living is a natural part of the motivation of a writer; but, on the other hand, there is often a passion: a passionately motivated truth to tell.

The first piece is called "My Words Bled"; and, in the drama of its opening words, is the distress of years of initial writing that seemed to spring from nowhere and grind down the writer into abandoning the spring from which they came. Discovering myself to be a writer did not come naturally; indeed, writing was one of many possibilities. In a certain sense, then, many failures made possible the success of succeeding to continue to write; and, in the process, there is beginning to emerge more of a definition to being a writer: of being a kind of anthropological explorer. Beginning with my own experience, writing is like finding that the psychological, philosophical and theological dimensions of human existence are expanding "shells": a kind of fluidly moving "energy of meaning" that seems to be one place and, at the same time, touches "all" other places. The words of this poem, then, reflect on that initial bleeding; but bleeding, if unchecked, leads to death: the death of a writer. Nevertheless, this was a beginning.

MY WORDS BLED

Like a too fruitful sapling: unstoppable.
I wrote too much and exhausted
the body of the spring in which they ran.

I fled like a snail from its shell.

Prematurely leaving home, I neither left it nor could rest in it;
and not inhabiting its purpose made me homeless:
a disordered upgrowing in an ingrowing unhappiness.

Like a surgeon operating on his own stomach -
but not a surgeon nor with a scalpel -
only a loose mirror and a home-made knife.

I fell underground.
Lying in the silence, desperate to do nothing;
doing nothing I did what nothing can do:
listening in the damp muddy warmth
and breathing in the sight of a shepherd's lamp.

I visited myself in the company of others
and suffered their incision.
I wrote again:

far fewer words fell
like footsteps in the autumn;
or the first winged leaves
of an acorn
outbreaking a scabby compost.

There are times when we seem to make progress in our life
and even find a routine that rounds out our daily effort and
tasks; but then, in the crumbling of resolve, the ever-present
weaknesses of life break out again and dissolve the almost

saving stability like a computer virus wrecking through a screen. But, at the time, it looks like we are on a rise and rising beyond the repetitions of life; and, while it lasts, it has a kind of blessedness about it – but a blessing that falls off as it lies like water on a stone or a pearl of dew on a leaf, all too ready to roll off to the unchaste touch of another.

DAY-BROKEN-BREAD

The morning-calling-blue
seeps up the edge of the
drawn down iodine black of night.

I rush between splashes,
too cold to cry, too wet to care,
and warmed in the cycling,
awash in the sweat and dripping shivers
until the tent-like cathedral
is suddenly there.

In the door-protected-stillness
the glow of the red, overhead heaters,
suspended in an off-white scarcely lit light,
casts an outstretched swathe
of firelight from the open-sided chapel
into the grainy grey space
that sits like a fog
in the building's cavernous, clothing silence.

Dawn drops down like a waterfall
through overhead shafts;
but noiselessly, speaking a purply hue.

The day's opening Eucharist and the hope,
inexplicable,
of a day to develop the day before

and not drive me,
once more,
to other places and people and work.

A training does not always come easily; indeed, it may not even be obvious that it is necessary because a certain kind of learnt insight has to start to take root to show us what it is that we are not doing. Over the years, then, it is not just about turning and returning to writing but making that appallingly slow progress which comes from repeatedly constructive criticism inching its way into consciousness as if, in a sense, it has to forge the tracks to do so bit by bit; indeed, to begin with, it is almost as if it was like writing through a structural blindness, a kind of word-structure ignorance that was almost impenetrably hidden in an unseeing sending of words through "gaps" in time. Perhaps one of the functions of tiredness and stress is the forestalling of learning, where learning is that acquisition of the sight of what we are doing through seeing what others have to say about it as if, at a certain moment, we unpeeled a perceptual blind-spot and saw, more clearly, the problematic sentence structure or its lack.

But there is, too, that striving after truth which is like building out of glass bricks, not an object we have made but a collection of insights we have found; indeed, it is as if the words are a kind of unpicked part of what exists that pass to the perceiver a glimpse of what is within: as if the impression itself is formed through an unveiling of what is there.

WORD-LIGHTS

Writing is like wrestling
time from chores,
eating, paying the rent, occasional jobs, courses, interviews
and trying to be a musician until the fantasy faded,
leaving the question-ever-remaining of what to do.

Writing returned,
and what wild hopes came from so little success;
and after such little success came
so many rejections.

Writing became essays,
sprawling works in need of structure and subheadings,
beginning the too-time consuming process of learning from
readers;
but time passes and what was too slow to acquire quickly,
the slowness of life supplied!

What we were too rushed to learn we learnt through the patience
forced upon us by failing to move forward from our failures.

Writing through the blizzard of facts
and impressions and seeing that the shape of our seeking and
searching is on the edge of being lost,
we head-down persevere in the course of crossing
to where we can seize the shape of what to say:

Words are a socialite,
identifying our identity and socialising the isolated
in the course of culture's company.

Searching for the light-words to turn inside out,
like a flowering phosphorescence,
the hiddenness undisclosed and almost seeking to be sought,

as if a goblet of light, flowering in the sunlight,
bespeaks a word awaiting to be said:

Truth is a socialite:
a friend to all
and a stranger to no one.

Writing is like finding a word,
His word,
while unsplitting,
making one word in all that exists:

giving the reason
faith finds in science
the image of itself.

Light is a socialite.
For we can see
when we are in it
that we are not alone.

Writing and returning to writing is like the compulsion of hoping to win a bet and betting, again and again, only to find that no amount of playing amounts to a position, a vocation or to earning the daily bread. How many writers have tried to earn a living from other work and failed, just as they have failed at writing, and yet have been unable to give up the trembling thought of the next piece and the hoped-for breakthrough? Wherefrom springs the delusion of success if not from an origin different from the failure of so many efforts? Writing must originate from another source to that of succeeding to sell it.

What "originates" writing? Is there, indeed, an explanation for being a writer any more than there is an explanation for being a "fish", or a "painter" or anything else? If it is within us to write then it was not planted by the writer; and, at the same time, rejecting it is like the fish unclothing its scales. Communicating is a key instrument in the psychological self-understanding of the human person: expressing the principle that putting experience into words unfolds who we are and develops our relationships to others. The "Word", however, is also the revelation of God: a "Word" spoken on a Holy Breath; indeed, even before we existed, there is the "Word" that is from all eternity: the mysterious expression of God from God in the eternal Son.

Thus, being a writer is both a gift and a sign of what points inwards and outwards to our origin. Returning to the poem, however, all this was far from clear and expresses the uncertainty of an uncertain pursuit of words.

THE GAMBLER

pulls on a one-arm-bandit
with the change on which he lives:
adolescent; spontaneous writing; correction fluid;
part-time worker; unhappy; manual work.

Years of "trying" dried the point of work to a
brittle dissatisfaction.

I do not know what to be;
and I cannot give up the question.
Either God is at work in the answer
or "giving up" is a "dying option" that I cannot do.

Studying more successfully; in print once; eventually paid.

But years of "trying-hours" changes time into an
uncertain sentence of waiting on replies and trying again.

Why write?

Why not go back to doing what did not earn enough to marry?

Why not go back to the building work,
learning on the job I never completely learnt to do?

Why not go back to the bending, over-lifting, I can no longer
support?

What hope is there of breaking new ground when time after time
the letter slaps the ground
out of which it grows?

Days, months and years of bitter drips of published pieces and
hoped for money; and courses; gifts; contacts; and unfounded
promises of progress.

The last coin, spent like a thrown dice, on the photocopy of a
poem.

Have you heard the "hurting words"
-published? paid? trained? -
that makes us spring out another message to the world in which
we work
as an unpaid
writer?

In this piece, marriage is decided upon and my fiancé and I
have visited the priest and he has asked me to get a job. When
I was considering the priesthood, I was also asked to get a job
and just carried on writing, earning a pound or two from a few
poems. So, when I was asked again to get a job and ended up
in a laundry a week later, it spoke to both me and my fiancé
that God is at work.

What follows, then, was originally a song that I wrote and
sang, twice, in the laundry canteen.

A BLUESY DAY

I have got to give up the writing
because it will not even pay for the lighting

and do what the priest said:
get a job, any job, to begin with –
if you want to get wed.
Because if marriage is not practical
then maybe, just maybe, it is not actual.
But what is the point applying
if time after time of trying
there is-a-no, there is-a-no denying.

But the very next day
– hey! not any day –
but the very next day
my "sister" rings
and I say: do I want to work where?

And so I wrote an end to writing
when I filled in the form for the job.

Then the day of the week,
from the day I proposed,
I was in Church on time to pray
when I came up and out of my way
it was hot and bright, and time was tight –
dressed to impress I borrowed a car
and arrived like a fallen star
to the interview
for the job in the laundry!

The manager said not to worry what you read
stay a week or a year, whichever is ahead.
And so I got the job in the laundry,
just in time for getting wed.

In the course of working in the laundry I developed a variety of illnesses, particularly bouts of pleurisy, during which I would dream that the laundry was coming through the bedroom; and, during these times of illness, as I had by now begun further studies, I would press out what I could in the time before returning to work. There came a point, however, when I had been given a grant to complete a book based on a short piece published in an academic journal; and, during that time of intense, if inconclusive writing, there developed a compound of illnesses which, together, brought me struggling to the doctor.

I WROTE

in the closing of the door.

First came the sneezing
the midnight shivers
followed by the cough,
the blistering lips,

and the time it took
to put the bin out
and the time it took
to recover breath.

I wrote while illness fell,
forcing me down like the first forward down
beneath the fallen scrum.

Then midway through the meal
I had to leave the table
never having ever
left my food unfinished.

Lowering myself to the bed
it started to go through my head
-blisters, fever, cough, lungs and leg –
are my clothes slipping off their peg?

What a mysterious conclusion
to my effort to earn our living -
landing upon this uncertain sand
of a life-threatening condition:
clotting in my leg and lungs,
pneumonia and pleurisy.
My wife and children visited.
It is hard to hide tears between visiting smiles and
to beg for the bills we were unable to pay.

But the door did not close

and I returned to write again,
to fight again,
for space to write again.

In "Word-Work", the first section is called 'Turning Words'; it was, to begin with, one of the possible titles of this collection. However, thinking about it further, turning words is a part of writing but not the whole of it. Indeed, considering that the turning of wood could be construed as an almost arbitrary imposition on the wood itself, it could follow that turning words is too emphatic about the time it takes to choose words; whereas, in reality, there is the impinging limitations of budget, reader and deadlines. Perhaps, though, the avoidance of "deadlines", of lines that merely repeat a previous thought, is a part of the task in that there is always a necessary search for a fresh expression, especially if I have been working on a theme for a long time, lest there be nothing vital in "today's work".

"Word-Work"

Part I: Turning Words

Words are not exactly stuck to things nor completely separate;
and, in the process of writing, there is re-wording:
as if getting closer to the subject is getting clearer
about what or who it is.

Simultaneously, words work within the person
and throughout the writer's subject;
indeed, is writing more about reading: reading which reaches into
the lived meaning that lies en-souled in experience?

"Word-Work" is an "inner" experience in an "outer" activity.

Asking where the sense lies is not about predetermining its
presence; but, like creation itself,
meaning flows through the parts and the whole.

Part II: "In Particular: Beached or Beginning?"

Stress unpredictably builds and builds, amassing an
explosive force that may collapse our lives:
a freezing that bursts the bottle;
a heating that implodes the
"I can";

or a growing disorientation that disfigures the shape of the day;

Or, alternatively, we may "read" the twitches in our eyes,
the chores undone or the "stressy" exchanges,
the sagging into a seat on the beach,
the non-read books and the multiplication of health problems.

It may be true that each of us needs to work

and that we need to study as well as to work more:

so each subject that is studied overspills with the others
to the point that we are swimming in overwork, deadlines,
extra reading, applications, project work, coursework,
exam schedules, a mass of poetry along with other
enriching visits to places until, finally, the cork blows and the
Champagne froths all over the place.

Or, alternatively, there is the "dropping a grade",
doing enough but not too much and passing up on all the extras.
Not to mention commuting and reading, writing and fitting in late
nights and early mornings, holiday time and "free" time,
family time and time that belongs to cleaning,
gardening and talking to the children;

and, of course, the complete mental absence from everything other
than the work-in-progress, the next dead-line or the
scheduling adjustments because of "slipping"
back further than the date of submission.

Or, alternatively, there is walking away at the end of the day from
the list of undone bits and pieces and into the piles, as it were, of
home-to-be-done "things" that spread, like cluttered rooms,
from draws and bins and table-tops and not put away clothes,
towels and toys; but, that walk between "work elsewhere" and
"work at home" cannot be too quick,
the distance is too great and it takes time to climb down from
"out there" to "in here" and the conflicting points of departure for
any number of needed activities.

But then there are the complications of workplace changes:

an email address disappears; positions altered to the point of
being unrecognisable; streamlined administration turns into
new line managers;

meetings which, unclearly, clear the way to changing everything
and leaving nothing.

Part III: "Meeting a Word"

Then, just as there was an answer to prayer in going to work,
in the prayer to leave, there is
taking leave of the reasons
to remain

and opening to the opportunity of leaving to do "Word-Work".

Now there is time to be "in" and time to be "out".

Writing each day,
wrestling to refuse to resist holidays,
albeit briefly drafting impressionistic moments which agglomerate
into prose.

A day's work includes weighing the cost of a conference
or wondering whether it is possible to write more, further afield,
or dig deeper in the questions which spreadeagle even further
than at first thought.

The challenge of the day, every day, is to take the work closer to
publication and payment.

The meaning of experience comes to meet me in the dialogue
between word and event; and, like Peter, it is time to listen to the
Lord and to

"Put out into the deep and let down your nets for a catch" (Lk 5: 4;
and cf. also Jn 21: 6).

God gives in taking away what no longer develops us.

Would we have it any other way?

It is deceptive, in a way, to think only of words functioning in the completion of a final piece of writing. Just as many conversations run on long after they are finished so there are messy splashes which arise out of the "landing" of a piece of writing. Thus "After-Words" is about that trail of ideas and reactions that both follow on from a particular work, very often return us to it and sometimes evaporate like steam or seed the beginning of another piece.

"After-Words" could also apply to what others have scattered through their thoughts and which have, like elemental ingredients, the possibility of springing up afresh in the soul of another's soil: that hidden, fertile place, within which the "new" begins before it breaks the surface and shoots up in the light and warmth of day.

AFTER-WORDS

I have often found that writing,
having grown like a whale,
leaves a trail
of small fish,
darting in the swell,
washed in the wet-sunlight,

bubbling,
dissolving in the air,
trailing traces of other thoughts:

burblings full of strangely attractive wordings.

Or a feeling of ideas spreading,
splintering, like glass, running, like splashes, escaping, like air,
their sentences –
but not lost,
more like circling

or ruminating about returning as another piece,
but in "another" moment.

Writing is not an entirely natural work:
hone it; hear it said; experience the throes of composition;
or is the subject more held in a gaze,
like a dancing partner loose and firm,
clothed in words we have woven and chosen
in our matrimonial making.

Writing, then, is a labour,
an act of word instead of word,
of word next to word,
of words written and rewritten, replaced, erased and rephrased.

If it is dry, dried in the handling,
water will not revive it –
fling it at the potter's pile
shattering and scattering
its opaque sense.

But if the words accomplish their sense,
the line is a drawing
and their sound a song
and their structure is
a transparently coloured sculpture.

We received through the giving of others,
so our giving reverberates back and forth:
drawing on others
and being drawn upon by others.

In the very development that was not possible
without what was bred in us,
we live the transmission of ideas through
the path to the truth which we
tread between us.

Those we know can sling an insult that sticks or works its way, like a screw, between cracked and vulnerable memories and reactions, sending us into an inner turmoil from which we need rescuing; and, at times, that rescuing is a word of reconciliation, a sacrament between God and man, outwardly receiving the love that heals and helps to quell the volcanic upset that blisters our imagination with raging replies. But there are times when, almost unaccountably, our hearts are weary beyond words, wanting a place of rest between problems, difficulties and disputes – a pause between crises to rest in prayers upon pleas and cries for help. Then there are other wounds, slighter in some ways, slipped into our hearts by strangers who, passing, pass a virus which unravels on its own and spreads an ever expanding fear of being a magnet of every kind of malice and collapsing us, hopelessly, into death or a transformation so dramatic that life blasts out against the desperate desire to die.

WITHOUT WORDS

I cannot describe
the crushing sensitivity
that unexpectedly bites,

when wounded with a word,
descending me
into the inescapable isolation of
the daylight dark:

alone under a beaming light.

I cannot describe
the arrival of an effortlessly unleashed
heat-seeking heart-wrecking word.

Without words
I cannot tell of how
the silence started to seal the stealing
of everyday life,
sending me to prayer,
or to the edge of railway tracks,
to join the people who suffer social suffocation.

Without words I would be dead.

REVOLVING DOOR[15]

How many times have I prayed and then stopped praying and then prayed again? How many times have I been into a church and then left, possibly not speaking to anyone or even knowing why I went in? How many times have I been to confession and confessed the same sins and left again, falling again and going back and then wondering why I went in the first place? How many times have I been to prayer groups, Mass, retreats, different denominations and even tried to help at these kinds of events and then left? How many times did I visit monasteries, convents, confessors, priests and advisors in the hope of I do not know what help?

Turning, up to a point, is good; but there comes a point when turning is about entering the door – but entering, in my experience, comes from God passing through the door and making it possible for me to go in.

---

[15] Robert J. Soper: https://unsplash.com/photos/uXtnyXgw_d8.

PART VII

CHRIST AND HIS CHURCH

Even for a baptized Catholic, brought up in a Catholic family and sent to Catholic schools, there is nothing automatic about the transmission and reception of faith. On the one hand there was the problem of my own reception of this faith, whether due to the experience of life or a questioning mentality which, in fact, remains a deeply helpful contributor to "receiving" this faith as a thought through word. On the other hand, perhaps I will never know the extent to which the prayer of my parents was more of a guiding influence on my life than all the sufferings and disasters that have otherwise been a part of it. In reality, though, the reception of this faith is not primarily about an "intellectual" appreciation of it; indeed, as fascinating and coherent as I find the relationship of "word" and "theological thought" to be, the real origin of my faith is that it was a gift. Faith was in fact given to me.

The mystery of being given faith is, in a sense, an intimate mystery of the shepherding of Christ. My relationship to Christ is not a relationship between equals. Christ had, as it were, visited me in many different ways and at many different times; but throughout all these different kinds of experience I was like an impermeable membrane: it was as if "nothing" had or could pass to me. Perhaps the nature of pride, hidden but real, is to reject the very advance that would heal it; indeed, choked as I was by my own emotions, I was always "looking" elsewhere to find answers: as if answers were like an antidote to an illness. The problem, however, that as helpful as human answers are to the mystery and challenge of suffering, they are like giving antibiotics to a drug resistant virus. In other words there is a radical insufficiency to our own efforts. How many years this painfully slow process of exhausting human effort has swallowed up? But, in a moment, I collapsed like a can imploding because of a vacuum: as if I finally "experienced" the lie of my own perfectibility – as if it were about my own insight, decision and act of will. Through the overwhelming evidence of being unclear about my vocation, unable to finish courses, unable to advance a working life, earn a living or renounce sin and the chaotic relationships which expressed it, I was suffocating from the preoccupation with myself and my own problems when the grace of God turned an "inwardness outward" and I believed in His help.

I did wonder, then, about reproducing here what was written elsewhere on the impossibility of marriage being made possible[16]; but, on reflection, perhaps a new work requires a renewed visiting of the experience. What follows, then, is a trilogy on the theme of exhausting human experience: Part I: The Endless Cycle of "Relationships"; Part II: the Psychological, Philosophical and Theological Answers; and, finally, Part III: The Answer of God in Action.

---

[16] Cf. Francis Etheredge, *The Family on Pilgrimage: God Leads Through Dead Ends*,
(http://enroutebooksandmedia.com/familyonpilgrimage/).

EXHAUSTING HUMAN EXPERIENCE (I)
"THE ENDLESS CYCLE OF RELATIONSHIPS"

Out of what unintelligible beginning begets the possibility of
turning to another?

The scarcely conscious seeking company
rebounding with embarrassment and becoming an introspective
nightmare examination of motives, inexpressible desires,
a kind of "homing in" as if driven by mechanical forces
uninformed by reading, real life interests and the reality of
ordinary, everyday friendships,
in which the self is fleshed out and made ready for
communication.

How many awkward moments of unskilled words,
linked to no news, no films, no events?
Compelled by a kind of raw attraction to company:
as if company is a kind of feeding ground –
a parasitic place "to be"?

Reading into a face, a kindness, a brief word -
a history of interest that was almost completely fictitious.

Coming from the edge of an entrance to a dance floor to dancing
through an intense self-conscious
electrical barrier to being in the presence of others:
as if "being alone" was a "repelling force" with lights and warning
sounds that rang so loudly in the ears that
I fled the feeling and failed to "pass"
from conspicuously alone to comfortably part of a group.

Then,
like a moth,
colliding with girls singed the wings and
confused, overburdened silences, turned advances

into retreats.

Gravitating to groups like orbiting debris,
not sure of why or what purpose and beginning to wonder at the
impossibility of passing into "company" when it led
to passing "through" company into loneliness.

Church and study groups like nets that caught the flotsam,
only to find the frustrations of an un-thought-through life
tearing at the too soon togetherness of premature "two-somes"
and pulling, like an asymmetrical swing,
sending me shying away from
stability and relational building.

Returning home after failure upon failure to find a future
different from the failing of past years and failing again
to get beyond the homing for home and conversational parents.

Gathering experiences but unable to gather friends;
and, in the process, almost losing those who were there
as passing through their lives was like
being a swirling down through a sea of messy brokenness.

But, like a word for the broken,
the cracked shell opens to a germinating word.

In the second piece of this trilogy, there are a few of the
insights which arose through questioning reality, study and
reflection; and, in a certain sense, these are a part of what
expresses our human identity: that we are in search of an
understanding that "makes sense" of our lives. This search,
then, draws on whatever makes us intelligible to ourselves;
and, as such, there is no natural limit to what can help us to
recognise the whole depth and breadth of human experience

which is, as it were, the cultural inheritance we discrimen-atingly assimilate.

The "places" from which we start may vary, both in terms of who began from where and from what question or observation we started and even from where we began in the different "moments" of our lives; and, therefore, there are many colourful strands to the history of these thoughts even if, in this account, the prose is relatively bare and unadorned with the detail of many experiences and insights. But, consider, on the one hand there was the memorable lectures on art history which showed how "embedded" a piece of work is in the times in which it was "made"; even if, in retrospect, the transition of an artist from realism to abstraction, has become a kind of "symbol" of a certain kind of progression or impoverishment. Maybe "truth" does need to be stated in terms of principles, like the principle of communication being behind the development of our self-identity through disclosing ourselves to others; but, too, maybe truth needs to be recovered in the concrete experience of what brought us to see what we are really like.

Perhaps, then, this is the point: that articulating what we have learnt about the human condition can have a "distance" about it; and, while it can be true, it maybe a type of truth that is almost like bone and lifeless (cf. Ez 37: 1-3): a kind of "distilled abstraction" that does not necessarily change anything or express a change in anything. Thus our insights may assemble somewhat mechanically and need, in the end, a different kind of dynamic to make them fruitful for life.

EXHAUSTING HUMAN EXPERIENCE (II) PSYCHOLOGICAL, PHILOSOPHICAL AND THEOLOGICAL ANSWERS

Psychologically
imperfect from imperfect predecessors,
our origin and formation is always through the reality of
parental imperfections.

Like a defective molecule clinging to what does not belong,
we complexify the past and charge it with destructiveness
that sharing would have disarmed;
and, like a depth charge,
it sounds a sprouting, sparking negativity
that damages human contact and
the updraft of memories,
obstructing the flow of what belongs to the fluid present and,
like a clotting in the channels of communication,
needs the pressure of the past-seeking-present to release it.

Philosophically
we are beings that need communication to breath;
and, just as we came to exist through others,
our identity is relational and needs dialogue to develop.

We are a whole,
wholly "form" and wholly "matter",
not a combination nor a juxtaposition but
like a meaning determining the sense of a word:

a word wholly central to a sentence and sensitive to
innumerable relationships.

As if ringed within rings and still a single ring,
our relationships run through our constitution

as cell structures through a tree.

Our bodily brightness glows with the splendour
of what is expressible in walking and talking, through gesticulation
and articulation of thoughts in words,
in dance, in song, through painting and music:
as if the score, the palette, the instrument
is begun in the depths of our being and overflows "outwards" with
what is "within".

Theologically
the "breath" is "visible" through the "life" of the body.

The vision founding our origin shows
through the relational nature of human being,
the mystery of the Blessed Trinity:
Three Persons in One God.

Just as the original gift of man and woman lost its lustre
and passed original sin down the generations,
so we were renewed in hope and help with the
Immaculate Conception
of Mary
and the redemptive coming of Jesus Christ,
so imperfection upon imperfection multiplied and mingled
with the grace of a relationship to God bringing renewal
through the Holy Spirit in the mystery of the Church.

Forgiveness re-founds the possibility of life.

In the last part of this trilogy, then, there is a sense in which getting "close" to the experience of the gift of faith is not excluding the communication of what it is but, in terms of the reality of human life, "enfleshing it" through recovering the "moment" of its existence. In other words, the process of reflection upon experience, which can and does enlighten us about our lives, illuminating the necessity of communication

116

for the psychological well-being of the individual person, is a kind of "expression" of our situation and not exactly a remedy for it. Nevertheless, there are, as it were, natural cures of psychological conditions; and, indeed, the remedying of an involuntary repression of childhood memories is a fact of my experience.

The experience I am now describing, however, is expressed in psychological terms in that I could not marry and then became capable of marrying; but, however, the nature of the experience was like the disciples experience of the risen Christ who "entered" a room, 'the doors being shut ... for fear of the Jews', and 'stood among them' (Jn 20: 19). In other words, it was not an initiative of mine that the words that I read changed me in a way that no words that I had ever read had ever done before. I knew, just as the disciples knew, that the room was locked; and, in that "moment", Christ's passing to me was what brought life: the belief that God exists and that He exists, as it were, to help me. Thus breath will enter you and cause the 'bones' to 'live' (Ez 37: 5), receive 'sinews', flesh and skin 'and you shall know that I am the Lord' (Ez 37: 6). In other words, being brought to life entails a renewal of the body, much as a marriage is a union of life and is expressed in the whole diversity of family life, work and prayer.

But it is not as if the "moment" remains a "moment"; rather, it multiplies down the years and becomes a beginning: a beginning that anchors a change that would not be there but for that "moment", like the "moment" of conception and the life that ever after lives.

EXHAUSTING HUMAN EXPERIENCE (III)
THE ANSWER OF GOD IN ACTION

Word-dust blows through us, settles, is swept away,
like soil in a field,
sandpapered wood, swept floors where people had trodden,
passing through, coming in and going out and leaving,
scarcely noticeable,
traces of life as it was lived and passed into dust.

One word stands forth and speaks of life as if it lives,
simply, memorably, insistently,
amidst the heat and tiredness of a pilgrimage and the impossibility
of finding direction, making a decision, discovering an outcome to
the interminable years
of searching between the possibilities of marriage and ministry,
multiple courses and their failures and successes,
moving, un-finding, through a maze of options:

a word that begets a real horizon of possibilities:
an old word brimming with promise:
a word true to itself and bringing what it says:
"I come to bring you life and life to the full" (Jn 10: 10).

But the word at first failed to find a hearing and remained,
like a background irradiation,
seeking a welcoming multiplication of meaning.

The Word found me unchanged and threw me out (cf. Mt 22: 13)
of the company of listeners to suffer an opening of the ear
through the pain that pierces the pride of self-sufficiency;

and, alone and in silence, thinking of the three prongs of a fork:
descending into madness, sin or suicide,

I listened to the words which came afresh to give me faith:

"If God can create everything from nothing then
He can give a new beginning to the sinner" (CCC, 298[17]).

One word, "go; and do not sin again" (Jn 8: 11),
ringing and singing
like chords of colours
completing and complementing each other,
opened the dead end of being unable to marry.

Words of the one Word present in the gift of marriage
turn water and its difficulties
into wine.

The following trilogy begins with a poem which was based, as it says, on a dream when 'I could not sleep'. I was staying in London, having gone on a "discernment-visit" to consider, along with others, the possibility of a vocation to the Catholic priesthood; indeed, it was one more visit in a life which had almost been "riddled" with the possibility of the priesthood: as if a "vocation" was a kind of infection and not in fact an expression of love. This "turn" to the Church again, however, had the character of a decisive turn: a turn to marriage; indeed, it emerged very clearly that the vocational trips to London were an opportunity to go out with various women. Thus, in the end, it was this fact of constantly looking for a wife that helped me to see, eventually, the need for an honest realism about what was expressed in the heart of my activity. In other words, whatever the possibility of there being a vocation to the priesthood, it was clear that the possibility of marriage was outrunning whatever had prompted it; indeed, as I recall, maybe the origin of the "idea" of the priesthood was

---

[17] Catechism of the Catholic Church, CCC, followed by the article referred to: CCC, 298.

more to do with not forming friendships and escaping relationships than with any kind of service. The gift of faith, then, healed the impossibility of being able to pass through the "barbed" gate to marriage; and, at the same time, it showed that the fear of an inescapable suffering needed a grace greater than the "natural" desire to marry.

The poem goes on to speak of 'the wild beasts' that 'drank themselves tame'; and, although it does not go into detail, the water is the *word of God* which, if graciously received, changes as it enlightens the 'wild beasts' that drink it.

A CRIB TRILOGY (I)
CHRISTMAS

I could not sleep
for dreaming
of when Christ
was made the fountain-head
of the well within the world
of God's grace;

and out-poured
a milk-white
lake of peace
in the midst of dead water.

On the inside edge of Heaven
wild beasts
drank themselves tame.

This second part of the *Crib Trilogy* was written after marrying and as the children came and started growing up amidst our life and monetary difficulties; and, in its way, it bears witness to how the "hype" of presents can really oppress parents and inflict all kinds of challenges on marriage, family life and the mystery of the event of Christmas. Whatever the particular characteristics of that "moment", I do remember that our Christmases are often blessed with my wife's ability to buy good presents on an often frustratingly tight budget and that we often receive bags of gifts from different people or organisations, including loads of biscuits and sweets; and, in the reality of the event of Christmas morning, there is often a sense of being amazed at how especially peaceful it was when, by comparison with the friends of our children, our celebration is simpler and more modest than many others.

I think the next piece, however, reflects more of the overshadowing of the trial of difficulties and the need for peace, beginning in my own heart.

A Crib Trilogy (II)
A Christmas Present

Part I

Xmas
is not a social disease
indebting us to credit cards, overtime
extremely extended opening hours –
all of which encourages an outrageous expectation
for what we do not want to buy,
cannot afford to buy
or do not really need to buy.

Xmas
is not a family complaint
that breaks out in divorce.

Xmas
is not a personal crisis
in which we are out on our own
without the gift of company.

Part II

And so I turn elsewhere,
to a different beginning,
almost unrecognisably connected,
before beginning again.

A walk in the quarry
is like looking to bridge the pass:
a shape to speak the start of a thought.

I do not want old words
of other poems
pieced together in a heap.
Neither can I force from the rock
a complete work from a phrase
that fell out of the air like a frosted fragment
splitting from what remains inaccessibly hidden.

Searching about I found a sound with a seam:

running back to the middle of the night prayer,
running down to the possibility of a word with which to begin,
running on to where only listening can lead.

Part III

Christmas
is the advent of peace:
Peace is coming in person.

Peace is a Person:

a Person between people,

a heart beat between hands held up
to drink a kiss,

bringing communion
destroying division.

Christmas advanced with the tension of chores
in making ready,
the shopping,
wrapped into presents,

but then relaxing in the walk to Church
and the time to think,
to pray and to receive the gift:

Christmas comes
to give
Christ to us!

In the next and last piece of this Christmas trilogy what
comes to the fore is the help to us, indeed to me, of the
mentality of our children.

Owing to the hassling buzz of winding up work, possibly
starting the Christmas chores in terms of driving back the
damp, or scrubbing it back, wrapping presents and the
incessant worries over who has what and whether he or she
will be happy with it, there is a point to walking to Church in
the middle of the evening to an early "midnight" Mass: the
whole point being the calming of the walk itself and the hope
that it helps us all to get a good sleep. Thus, our custom of
going to Mass on Christmas Eve and then, by the time we have
had mince pies and a cup of tea and walked home again, it is
late enough for the youngest children to be going to bed. The
following morning, then, my wife and I have arranged the

dining room with the table in front of the crockery cabinet and covered with a needleworked cloth. The crib, visible on the top of the cabinet, and a semicircle of chairs opposite, each with a pillowcase underneath, containing presents, allows us to gather, hear a word from a Gospel and sing to begin the day. Thus, a Christmas morning prayer is followed by the first opening of presents which, customarily, goes on for a few days as the children have bought presents too.

A CRIB TRILOGY (III)
THE CHILDREN'S GIFT

Is unwrapped and visibly present,
lying in the fearfully hoped for appreciation
of almost nothing
that amounts to
almost
everything:

of being together;
reading;
playing;
welcoming another;
and praying over a shared meal.

Having knelt in front of an empty crib,
recalling our difficulties of finding affordable,
desirable presents,
and remembering the others who help,

I can see the gift of Christmas
lies in the mystery of
the children's gift:

of being happy with what they are given.

The next poem was not written until long after the experience of going from Christian denomination to Christian denomination in a kind of semi-conscious search in response to the various comings of Christ; indeed, it seemed very clear that Christ expressed a fullness of humanity which was like the goal of all human development but, at the same time, it seemed like He was a complete mystery and almost unintelligibly "unconnected" to my own life and sufferings. Nevertheless, the image on which this poem was founded came to "make sense" of my many visits to different forms of Christian worship and fellowship. At the time, I was not able to go beyond the "doorway" of the Church and to "belong" or indeed to participate in what appeared to be only "patchy" and partly recognisable expressions of our human reality; indeed, I would now say, that these visits, for all their occasional human warmth, were like pieces of a puzzle out of context and did not really makes sense until I saw 'Several ships form an arrow in flight'.

ECUMENISM

One Church
flies through space
like an arrow-illuminating-darkness.

Several ships form an arrow in flight:
each on the edge of nothing;
each on the edge of each other;
and each on the leading edge
of the arrow in flight.

Several ships in the
shape of Christ
the arrow-head:

one Church
- the Catholic Church -
subsists at the point of unity
in the One Church.

One Church
- the Church of Christ -
sails like a fleet
through the darkness.

The picture and the poem below are based on the sculpture of an angel by my late father, Peter Howard Etheredge; and, while I have never seen an angel, the possibility of its existence is appealing. A being in broken light, not because light is broken but because the three-dimensional light fills space and sparkles; it is a whole, but a dynamic whole, instantly transporting itself in a shimmering brilliance. At the same time, almost contradicting myself with two accounts of the same phenomenon from different points of view, the angelic being is not in time and space unless, like a companion, "his" mission is in our midst (cf. Tobit).

An angel stands above materiality as much as energy is immersed in it; and, therefore, an angel expresses the "upper limit" on a scale of being that "descends" to the depths of matter. The meaning of the word angel, as messenger, entails the definite sense of a "go between"; and, as such, gives the impression of "passing" between us and God. At the same time, just as we are individuals in the midst of a community of relationships, and yet we can bear a message to one another, so no doubt angels are not just "functionaries" but the bearers of a distinct individuality: a unique "beingness" that we will not discover until we meet when the invisible becomes visible.

Therefore, on death, I hope to travel from the depths of the ocean to the limits of the farthest flung galaxies, passing every kind of stellar wonder in the process, all in the company of my guardian angel; who, I would hope, would accompany me into the presence of God, literally holding my ethereal hand as I encounter the loving mercy of Christ Himself.

AN ANGEL

descends like a
squatting squirrel
in prayer.

Its origin like a root
in its shape:
curling out from a centre
in its base
as if engulfed
is the self-expression
of Being itself.
But all of this is half-hidden
to the sculptor's
opening out the shape in the wood;
and words express what could not be said
without the act of carving to ignite them.

The angel fell as if falling
from on High
is like the flight
of dripping fire:

Drawn out in the burning down,
elongated in descent,
it drops in the love
out of which it flamed
and fills the pool with peace.

Guardian Angel
of ours,
seen in the scattered
patches of light
thrown across a dark room
- pray for us
to leap alight
at the burning
end of day.

Amen.

A gift is well wrapped, attractive and a thoughtful expression of the giver; and, at the same time, there is a "moment" to give: a birthday; an anniversary; or on getting married. The present is "within" and, at the same time, the outward expression of it is a promise of what is good. There is, in the words which express our giving, a natural "liturgy" which celebrates an irrevocable "opening" in the giving and receiving of the gift.

We have received the gift of ourselves from God; and, pondering the fact that each one of us is a gift, leads us to think of God as "Gift from Gift". Just as the Father gives himself wholly to the Son and the Son, together with the Father, give themselves wholly to the Holy Spirit, so God gives himself wholly to us; and, in God giving himself wholly to us, he brings to life the possibility of giving ourselves wholly to him and to each other in the mystery of marriage.

But just as God does not take back the gift of himself, so the giving of himself in Jesus Christ and his Church renews the original gift of man, male and female; and, in the renewal of redemption, lies the renewal of the celebration that each one of us is a gift to be given.

Even if, in the language of married, everyday life, there are many ordinary expressions of everyday actions there is, nevertheless, the expression of a great mystery. Just as each one of us "recapitulates" the beginning so each marriage communicates the mystery of God through the union of Christ and His Church.

"The Domestic Church", then, was written early on in my married life and bears numerous traces of the struggles of coming to marriage and the welcome of children when already forty! When we were away on retreat, a retreat on which we had to take our five children with us, I remember the sheer agony and exhaustion of tiredness and the recurrence of a back complaint; and, therefore, when we arrived at the Eucharist on the Sunday morning, it was as a wreck of tiredness. In the Gospel, however, Christ walks on the water and calls to Peter to get out of the boat and come to Him; and, as we know, Peter got out of the boat and started to walk and then to sink but Christ clasped him by the hand and rescued this man of 'little faith' (Mt 14: 31).

In that Eucharist I was able to straighten up and bless God for help and, at the same time, I always thought of this word as an encouragement to evangelise: to get out of my comfortable "boat" and to walk towards Christ. In retrospect, I see how this call to get out of the boat was also an invitation to walk on the waters of death and to have more children; and, as we went on to have three more children, I see this "word" as being fulfilled in the impossibility of bearing with the daily work of bringing up a young and growing family of eight close together children.

THE DOMESTIC CHURCH
Part I

Communication or matri*moan*ing?

Talking is a daily act of married life:
sometimes it is easy, sometimes it is not.

As when our daughter swims upon delight at the sight and sound
of paper crumpled off the parcel and flung about the air.

Or when gloom has glued my wife's lips until solvent tears
roll away the boom lying all the while in my very own ears.

A marriage begins with a word
and continually opens with each being heard.

Part II

The welding "I do" is a work to do.

So two into two makes cooking for you and cleaning for me.

But sharing is not half the caring
because work is no rail line when illness and birth plough
into the plan
making flexible the family man.

For if a marriage is not practical is it actual?

Part III

Prayer is to being one what lungs are to breathing,
so praying together exercises staying together.

And just as marriage is made in heaven while it is lived on earth,
it needs fruit to flower as well as roots and manure to suit.

Part IV

Now a word to end on irritation:

it is the oyster's grip
on the gift of grit
which makes a fine pearl,
set in tradition,
a true condition
of peace in the whirl.

Part V

A concluding thought:

A tree in the wood is not so wind blow as a tree on its own –
the support that strengthens stability in the storm
is also a place to shelter –

just as a town is a gathering of houses,
so each family is a 'domestic' Church, gathered together
in the *Church of Christ*.

We are surrounded by imagery, as it were, as if the very existence of the universe is a kind of "metaphorical expression" of the mystery of the Creator; and, at the same time, not just the Creator but the whole mystery of the Blessed Trinity: the Being-in-Relationship "who" originates all relationships.

Whether it is water, rock, bread, wine, valleys, mountains, goats, sheep or snake, there are innumerable ways that the language of creation, including what men and women make, is transformed in the telling to communicate what is in the heart and mind of all of us. Indeed, even before the words of the writer, the paint of the artist or the shape of the sculptor, the sound of the musician or the scent of perfume, there is the "original" brilliance of what exists. My eldest son remarked recently, almost as if puzzled: "Why is the setting sun so beautiful?" Does creation not speak, then, of the "original" beauty of the Creator; and, as it were, of the origin of every good gift? Thus there is both what exists in the reality of our lives and is there through our fault and there is, too, what exists in the fruitfulness of a life through the passing fecundation of the grace of God.

Even what seems to be a "solitary flame" cannot but exist except in the context of the wick or other fuel, the prior lighting, the oxygen needed for burning and the whole context of the universe and its characteristics expressed in the rising of the flame, its fluttering colours and plumed existence; indeed, thinking of the "tongues of flame" that appeared on the disciples heads at Pentecost, it is almost impossible to imagine what else could have expressed the visibility of what makes communion between us possible: the "Holy Spirit". Perhaps marriage, the *Domestic Church*, is a hearth of this love.

OH FLAMING FIRE

strung between candlewick and sun,
swollen at the base like
a bulb at the point of growth,
stretched out skyward like a body's breath
and still, still, and still flickering;

struck as a note only audible to the eye,
like a trembling paint brush you mirror in the mirage
the mystery in your Maker:

a barely visible shimmering
shining through creation's imaging of the

Being of the Blessed Trinity.

Oh Flaming Fire,
You dropped in the hearth of spousal love
the place for fire:
a grate within which love love's to dwell,
warming while heating the household
and burning the fuel
that belongs to husband and wife.
Wild fire rages like desire and destroys!

But love loves to be at home
and thrives on the joys
that beget the blaze
that burns off the
discolouring greys.

Oh Flaming Fire
feed the heart
that brightens the light
of family life!

The penultimate piece in this collection could well have been the first in that it poses the basic questions of an unresolved life. The date on it, however, was the 7th of October, 1997, almost a year after marrying. Either, then, this is the date it was rewritten, or I wrote it in view of the questions which had tormented me for over twenty years. Indeed, thinking about it now, I am inclined to the view that it was written earlier than marriage because of marrying being an amazing change from uncertainty, indecision and the impossibility of marrying: of crossing an irrevocable chasm.

Why, then, not rearrange the book and put this poem at the beginning? The main reason is not to leave the reader with the sense that everything is finished; rather, to leave the reader in the "framework", as it were, of the questions and prayers that expressed my life for so long. In other words, just as my life has not stood still in all the turning and turning again, so it is possible that ending with prayer is like extending an invitation to others to go on hoping the impossible hope of a new beginning.

LET US PRAY

to God our Creator Father,
His reconciling Son
and the helping Holy Spirit.

Part I

We pray to the Father
to the origin in God of all beginnings
- to the architect builder whose labouring leads to rest –

to answer the question in our making:
Did you make men and women?

Answer me.

What gifts did you give in the gift of a man?

Answer me.

What gifts did you give in the gift of a woman?

Answer me.

What do I do in society?

Answer me.

Do you want me to marry or minister in Church?

Answer me.

Tell me, if you made me, who I am.

Part II

We pray to His Son
to reconcile men to their manhood
and women to their womanhood;
to turn the married man into a husband
and the married woman into a wife;
to turn the husband into a father
and the wife into a mother
and their offspring into children;
to turn the old to the young,
and for the young to grow old;
to turn the rich to the poor,
the doctor to healing,
the lawyer to *the Law,*
the nurse to the dying
and the priest to preaching
the Son's reconciliation of His brothers and sisters to their Father.

Part III

We pray to the Holy Spirit
to ignite our days of darkness
and to burn out into the light
the gratitude that died within us
like frozen coals in the clinging wet;
to bring to life the good of life;
and to put an end to the deadening end
of disguising the sin at the heart of conversion.

Where will the crucifixion of Christ end?

In the unborn, the unwanted, the unwell, the elderly, the infirm
and which we, in our turn,
will become one day?

If we do not preserve our humanity in the help we give to others,
then we are helping to harden its arteries.

God help us to have faith in the hope His love is stronger
than the death in which we are drowning.

What is evangelization? It is announcing that God exists and loves to help us; and it is announcing this in the facts of our lives: in the witness of being open to life and having eight children, finding work, publishing books, enduring the difficulties of unemployment, illness and rejection and still being able to celebrate the providential gift of marriage, family life and the daily help of the Lord.

But there is, too, that coming together in the Church and going out, as a part of it, to celebrate the love of Jesus Christ for sinners, beginning with our own witness to His loving forgiveness and help. At the same time, however, as we share what God is doing with us we know that receiving this word is beyond our power to give it; and, therefore, we pray that God makes possible the passing of His love to others when, in what way, according to the mystery of His will, He will do so.

EVANGELIZATION

is God at work in creation through
a giving in the receiving which leaves
us different from before.

Believing what we saw,
in the word we received,
makes beginning the good,
which fear had forbidden,

an end to the sins of escaping
the entrance to marriage
in the moment of marrying.

Passing through the barbed door (cf. (cf. Jn 20: 19)
peels the suffocating self sufficiency,
shedding the inability to suffer the loving of others.

Painfully passing more deeply through the thorned gate
that forbids retreat and seeds the slowly growing thawing
that needs to meet the needs of others
in the daily life of husband and father
we meet the Mother of God who tells her Son
of the wine we need (cf. Jn 2: 3).

What wonder is it to behold that a man marries?
unless you know the twenty years of striving
that ceased one morning in the autumn sunshine
and began a life unlived until then in the newness of marriage.

Passing through the door closed to you
is not possible except through Him
who passed through the door closed through fear (cf. Jn 20: 19)

to announce

The Love that loves to love.

Evangelization is witnessing to the Word spoken from the
beginning and coming again in the work of re-creation
to continue to the end of a life lived,
if possible,
in turning to God.

Each fact of help being gathered to be scattered,
far and wide,
bringing a catch on the ever dawning tide

of the fishermen rescuing the needy (cf. Mt 4: 19; Jn 21: 11).

Who can destroy the root of destruction without being
destructive?

If a word-act can open,
in our hearts,
like an acid kissing blossom,
implanting a pain-seeking appetite,
severing us into enemies,

then what will return the bright begetting strength
of married loving,
restore the paved peace prepared for us in the past,
turn an enemy into a friend?

Evangelization is being open
to the wind which seeds the passing
through closed doors and opens
an unopened life to

the extravagantly blossoming brightnesses spreading
through the many facts abreast the breeze,
filling the horizon with the fullness that
completes the unfolding of the company
that comes together
to splash about and shout about,
the coming of the Son!

ABOUT THE AUTHOR

Mr. Francis Etheredge is married with eight children, plus three in heaven. He is the author of Scripture: A Unique Word, and a trilogy From Truth and Truth (Volume I-"Faithful Reason"; Volume II-"Faith and Reason in Dialogue"; Volume III-"Faith Is Married Reason"), all of which are published by Cambridge Scholars Publishing; The Human Person: A Bioethical Word (published by En Route Books and Media, 2017) is immeasurably enriched and complemented by Forewords from eight writers: one to the book as a whole and one to each of the seven chapters." The Family on Pilgrimage: God Leads through Dead Ends (published by En Route Books and Media, 2018) demonstrates how the gift of faith transformed agonies of searching into a decision to marry, work, unfold a family life, and witness to the help of God.

Francis is currently a freelance writer and speaker and his "Posts" on LinkedIn can be viewed here. Poetry; short articles; autobiographical blog; excerpts from books; and "Philosophize: A Ten Minute Write." He has earned a BA Div (Hons), MA in Catholic Theology, PGC in Biblical Studies, PGC in Higher Education, and an MA in Marriage and Family (Distinction). Enjoy these additional articles by Francis Etheredge:

- Witness "begets" Witnesses
  http://www.hprweb.com/2015/02/witness-begets-witnesses/
- Love is a Liturgical Act
  http://www.hprweb.com/2016/02/love-is-a-liturgical-act/
- The Holy Family, Celibacy, and Marriage: A Reflection on the "Passage" from the Jewish Rite of Marriage to the Sacrament of Marriage
  http://www.hprweb.com/2014/08/the-holy-family-celibacy-and-marriage-a-reflection-on-the-passage-from-the-jewish-rite-of-marriage-to-the-sacrament-of-marriage/
- "Do-it-Yourself" or Vocation: Coincidence or Providence
  http://www.hprweb.com/2015/10/do-it-yourself-or-vocation-coincidence-or-providence/